Expectations
Psalms 57:7

COLLECTION OF
LOW FAT & NO FAT RECIPES

by
Sally Mosier
and
Tennie Goen

Published by

Expectations
Psalms 57:7

PO Box 1902
Plainview, Texas 79073

EXPECTATIONS LOW FAT & NO FAT COOKBOOK
COPYRIGHT © 1995 by Expectations
ISBN 0-9651423-0-2

by Sally Mosier
and Tennie Goen
PO Box 1902
Plainview, TX 79073

Published by Expectations
PO Box 1902
Plainview, TX 79073

Editor: Tennie Goen
Designer: Sue Terry
Cover: DesignWorks Studio, Lubbock, TX

Printed in United States of America
First printing: 1995-20,000
Second printing: 1996-25,000

This book is dedicated
to my life time love,
my husband, Phil Mosier.

Phil, you loved me when I weighed 276 pounds, you loved me in the transition and you love me now. You have allowed me to be totally dependent on you and then allowed me to become totally dependent on God. I know it has been very difficult on you but the new Sally loves you even more. Thank you honey, for being willing to invest in my dream and test it and me with fire. A stronger yet more yielding vessel has emerged.

Special Thanks

❖ Tennie Goen, my right arm. When God gave the vision of *Expectations* to me He assured me that He would anoint people to come along side. I am seeing that assurance become a reality with you my dear friend. Thank you so much Tennie, for filling in the gaps in so many areas. You have been with me through the birth pangs and at times, even worse, the growing pains. You have organized me, balanced me, and stood with me. You have added so much to *Expectations* and to my ladies. Your hours of hard work and constant prayers have truly blessed us all. You have joined with your heart in the main objectives of *Expectations*, number one, to glorify God and number two, to help my ladies. Everything you are doing speaks to these objectives. I thank God for calling you and equipping you to be in the trenches with me. You have made them not quite so deep and harsh.

❖ Jean Tippery, my Mom, thanks to your success of losing 85 pounds at age 75, you have become a shining example that we all can lose weight at any age.

❖ Paster John Benefiel of Church of the Rock, Oklahoma City, Oklahoma, thanks for guidance on how to pull together and balance a ministry/business. Your knowledge and anointing have truly been a blessing to Phil and I.

❖ Pastor Billy Nickell of the First Assembly of God, Canyon, Texas, thanks for being my friend and for recognizing the anointing on *Expectations* from the start. Thanks for opening up your fellowship hall for my ladies to meet weekly.

❖ Tony Privitt, former agent/publicist to Lewis Grizzard, thanks for being the first "Professional" to believe in my vision. Your encouragement has blessed my life and added professional clout to *Expectations*.

❖ Frances Foster, our prayer warrior, only God knows the total effect of your prayers for *Expectations* and my family. Thanks for your strength and words of encouragement.

Acknowledgments

There are many people I would like to thank, without whose help, encouragement and inspiration this recipe collection would not have been possible. To the following people, I send my sincere appreciation.

- ❖ My ladies, as I so fondly call the members of *Expectations*, who so freely shared their recipes. This recipe collection was born out of their contagious enthusiasm.

- ❖ Joan Fore, the "Recipe Lady," as she is now known by all of our *Expectations* members. Without her help this recipe collection would have never happened. Thank you for all the hours of labor in the kitchen and on the computer. Joan has spent countless hours converting our members favorite recipes into incredible great tasting low fat dishes.

- ❖ Sue Terry, a long time friend, has also been a special friend to *Expectations*. Sue graciously extended her time, heart, and expertise to me when *Expectations* was in its infancy. Sue's creative work on the computer is present in our beautiful logo, brochures, and cover pages of this recipe collection.

- ❖ Jeannita Higginbotham, my sister, Ned, special thanks to you for being my most effective billboard. Your 65 pound loss has been an inspiration for many other success stories.

- ❖ DesignWorks Studio - Lubbock, Texas, thanks to Travis Patterson and Jason Vaughn. You guys are great! Travis, you were with me from the beginning helping to give form to my jumbled thoughts. Jason then you came on board, and the two of you developed my beautiful cover. I love it!

Expectations

Psalms 57:7

BEFORE

AFTER

Meet *Sally Mosier*, founder of *Expectations Freedom Weight Loss Plan*. Sally has lost 122 pounds and has successfully kept it off for nearly three years. Sally and her staff train their clients in low-fat eating. "Freedom" is the key word at Expectations. There are no expensive foods or supplements to buy, no measuring and weighing of food, nor calories to count. Expectations freedom weight loss plan includes, encouragement, motivation, and accountability. Sally and her staff personally work with clients to develop an individual eating plan. Expectations also trains you how to shop, to convert recipes, and to eat out successfully. Expectations is not a "diet," *it's a new way of life*.

If everything you've tried has failed, like it had for Sally, then what are you waiting for?

Call now and let Sally and her staff restore your "expectations".

1-800-795-1841

Everybody's Talking

"Twenty plus years of book publishing and entertainment marketing gives me a keen perspective of how difficult it is to sell over 20,000 cookbooks in West Texas and to have done it with no prior experience is nothing short of phenomenal. I see tremendous potential in your book and program. When you find the right media outlet to reach your audience, I can only wonder if your "expectations" can possibly be set high enough!"

    Tony Pivett
    Publicist/Agent, Lubbock, Texas

"After hearing the account of the wonderful work of God in Sally, we sought to have her on our show. We found Sally to have a heart to give God the glory for the obvious changes that have come about through her weight loss journey. As it is painfully clear to all of us, many Christians are struggling for victory in the area of their eating habits. The desire is strong, but the flesh is weak. We feel Sally Mosier has a valid place of service to the body of Christ."

    Larry and Sue Scoggins
    Host of "The Light Of The Southwest",
    Prime Time Christian Television, Midland, Texas

"Words cannot express the appreciation the women of Montgomery Blvd. Church of Christ have for the wonderful "Freedom Weight Loss Workshop". Your work truly glorifies the Lord because you are so inspired by His holy word and so willing to let others share in your success. I just know that other churches could benefit from your workshop and selling your cookbook as a fund raiser. The ladies are raving about the recipes and are buying extras as gifts for friends and family. You are right. It really is a "Freedom Weight Loss Plan".

    Donna Estes
    Montgomery Blv. Church of Christ Ladies Program Coordinator
    Albuquerque, New Mexico

"Her Christian based business is unquestionably a ministry and a blessing in the lives of many who have tried it all, and failed. Expectations is unique in that women from all denominations and even many of the unchurched are seeking Bible based council and instruction from Sally and her staff."

    John M. Benefiel, Pastor
    Church On The Rock, Oklahoma City, Oklahoma

"I am writing to recommend Sally Mosier and her weight-loss plan "Expectations". Sally has been a tremendous blessing to several ladies of our congregation and of our community. Since Sally has been large most of her life, she understands the pain these ladies feel and is able to minister to them in a special way."

    Billy D. Nickell, Pastor
    Fantastic First Assembly of God, Canyon, Texas

"The 12 week "Freedom In Eating" workshop that is offered by Expectations has been a super blessing in our congregation. The sessions are inspirational, and there is a true compassion that comes forth. I highly recommend the "Freedom In Eating" workshop to any congregation or anyone that is wanting to lose weight as well as keep it off for a life time."

> Steve Rogers, Pastor
> Trinity Fellowship Church, Plainview, Texas

"I am a very active mother of three young children. I had tried a few diets but I always seemed to starve. So I just gave up and resigned myself as being fat. When I opened Expectations door it wasn't like any other weight loss place I had been before. Sally was invigorating and she honestly cared. As the weeks went by the weight started coming off. One, two, and three pounds a week, I was happy. Every time I went to Expectations there was Sally with her encouragement and great advice for the week ahead. Sally and Expectations has changed my life and my views about eating. I plan on staying with this way of eating the rest of my life. As Sally has always told me, "Don't ever let yourself give up!"

> Tammy Kelley
> Expectations Weight Loss Member, Lubbock, Texas

"As I look back at my past "expectations" I can see why I was not successful at losing weight before. My motives were not acceptable before the Lord. With new motives, and not thinking of myself so much, God lead me to Sally and Tennie. I was successful in losing 35 pounds. The most helpful thing Tennie has trained me with is to let food have its proper place in my life. This summer, as I walked along the beach at the lake, wearing my swimsuit, I noticed my shadow on the sand in front of me. This shadow had indention's above the hips – an actual waistline – which I had not seen in a very long time. As a smile erupted across my face, I tingled inside and shouted, "Thank you God!" Thank you Sally and Tennie!"

> D'Lynn Morris
> Expectations Weight Loss Member, Lockney, Texas

"I have recommended this plan to a number of my patients to help encourage them in the lifestyle of a low fat diet."

> Terry Gage, M.D.
> Lubbock, Texas

"Your weight loss program is virtually identical to my post-coronary program, which turned out to be weight loss as well."

> Dick Sleeper
> Dick Sleeper Distribution, Sandy, Oregon

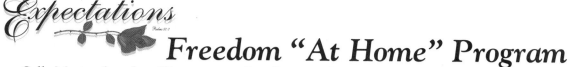

Expectations

Freedom "At Home" Program

Sally Mosier, founder of Expectations Freedom Weight Loss Plan, wants to let you know of an exciting new program called Freedom "At Home". The Freedom "At Home" Program has been birthed out of the requests of many people for an Expectations clinic to be opened in their home town.

Freedom "At Home" is an opportunity for those who are interested in losing weight but feel like they need support and encouragement from a Christian perspective. We are offering this 12 week program by mail. The first week you will receive the Enrollment Packet, which includes Sally's Freedom Weight Loss Plan booklet. You will also receive a weight and measurement chart, cooking hints, no and low fat product list, information on how to read labels, and basic "Getting Started" recipes and food suggestions. Everything you will need to get started losing weight will be included. There are no expensive foods or supplements to buy, no lengthy meetings to attend, and no measuring or weighing of foods. Freedom is the key word at Expectations. You will not be starting *another* diet that will lead to *another* failure. Expectations is not a "diet," *it's a new way of life*. The following eleven weeks you will receive all the material that we give our members who come to our clinics for their weekly sessions. These packets will be full of scripture, motivational material, recipes, nutritional and cooking hints. You will also receive three monthly newsletters and three monthly recipe collections. In order for you to experience the accountability that we all need, a stamped, self-addressed envelope and form will be provided in your second packet. Each time we hear from you, we will put another envelope in the next return packet. This will allow you to communicate your weight loss, measurements, concerns, questions, etc. Of course you may at any time pick up the phone and call us!

We are excited to be able to provide you with this twelve week Freedom "At Home" Program for the affordable cost of $50. It is our desire at Expectations that you will be able to walk in freedom in this area of life. If you have that same desire and are interested in us teaming up with you for the next three months, let us hear from you.

"Freedom Home Package Offer"

❑ Yes! I want to take advantage of your new Freedom "At Home" Package.
            Enclosed is my check or money order for $50.00.
❑ Yes, I would like a cassette tape of the Freedom In Eating Food Plan so that I will have a thorough understanding and get off to a great start! I have enclosed an additional $5, making my check or money order $55.

Name _____

Address _____

City _____ State _____ Zip _____

Phone _____ - _____

Make check payable to:
Expectations
P.O. Box 1902
Plainview, TX 79073

Freedom In Eating Seminars

These exciting seminars are taught by Sally Mosier, founder, of *Expectations* Freedom Weight Loss Plan, and Tennie Goen, director of curriculum. Tennie, a long time "fat" friend of Sally's, joined her in this journey with the Lord over a year and half ago. They both have experienced freedom in the area of overeating. Sally and Tennie not only have a shared vision, they have complementary giftings that the Lord uses as they present this wonderful message of hope.

If you are interested in your church hosting a *Freedom In Eating* Seminar, call: 1-800-795-1841.

Contents

FREEDOM GOES ON 83

My Favorite Recipes

Have you ever tried a new recipe and then forgot which cookbook it was in the next time you wanted to repeat it? Maybe you knew which cookbook it was in but you couldn't remember the name of the recipe! This page is for you to record the name of the recipe, the page number and results for easy reference the next time you want to repeat a favorite recipe

Sally and I have marked some of our favorite recipes throughout the cookbook. We hope you enjoy the exciting new way of life that low-fat cooking can bring.

Tennie

Name of Recipe	Page Number	Comments/Results
_____	_____	_____
_____	_____	_____
_____	_____	_____
_____	_____	_____
_____	_____	_____
_____	_____	_____
_____	_____	_____
_____	_____	_____
_____	_____	_____
_____	_____	_____
_____	_____	_____
_____	_____	_____
_____	_____	_____
_____	_____	_____
_____	_____	_____
_____	_____	_____
_____	_____	_____
_____	_____	_____

"My heart is fixed O God, on thee…"
Psalms 57:7

Appetizers

and

Snacks

TURKEY CHEESE ROLL-UPS

2 packages no-fat cream cheese

2 bunches green onions chopped finely (some tops)

2 cloves minced, pressed garlic

12 oz. turkey deli-thin slices

Mix the ingredients until blended. Spread on thin slices of turkey, roll up and chill.

Serves 10 to 15   Fat: 1 grm per serving

HAM ROLL-UPS

12 oz. sliced deli-thin ham   Fat-free cream cheese

Green onion

Spread thin sliced 99° fat-free ham with fat-free cream cheese. Place green onion on end and roll up. Slice 1/2-1/4" and place on pretty platter. Serve at Holiday meals.

Serves: 10-15   Fat: 1 grm per serving

TEXAS TRASH

4 c Corn Chex   4 c Rice Chex

1 1/2 c Fat-free pretzels

Layer ceral and pretzels spraying each layer with butter flavored Pam. Sprinkle Pam with powdered Worchestershire Seasoning and seasoned salt. Butter Buds may be added for more flavor. Bake 1 hour at 250°. Stir every 15 minutes and spray with Pam after each stirring. Add more seasoning if needed. Worchestershire sauce liquid can be used. Snackwells Cheddar Crackers are very good added to this.

Fat: .5 grms per serving

BAKED TORTILLA CHIPS

Use fat-free flour or corn tortillas. Cut into wedges, place on cookie sheet in a single layer. Bake at 350° for 8 to 10 minutes for flour or 10 to 15 minutes for corn. Sprinkle with salt or seasoned salt before baking.

Fat: 0 grms per serving

HOT SAUCE DIP

2 c Fat-free sour cream

1/2 c finely diced tomatoes

1 small finely diced jalapeño (can be omitted)

1 small can diced green chilis

1 t cumin

1/2 t garlic, minced

1/4 c diced onion

1/2 t oregano

1 T chili powder

Mix together and chill.

Yield: 2 1/2 to 3 cups   Fat: 0 grms per serving

TEX MEX LAYERED DIP

2 cans pinto beans (15 oz.) rinsed and drained

1 16 oz. carton fat-free sour cream

1 pkg. taco seasoning mix

1 1/2 c finely shredded lettuce

l large ripe tomato, chopped

1/4 c green onions

1/2 c shredded no-fat cheddar cheese

carrots, celery sticks or baked tortilla chips

Favorite

In medium bowl mash beans. (Put in microwave for 2 to 3 minutes first and the beans will mash easier and better.) Stir in 1 cup sour cream and taco seasoning mix. Spread bean mixture on a large serving plate. Spread remaining sour cream over bean mixture. Sprinkle with lettuce, tomato, green onion, and cheese. Serve with carrots, celery, or tortilla chips.

Yield 24 servings   Fat: 1 grm per serving; Tostitos Baked Chips 1 grm fat

EASY BEAN DIP

1 can Black Beans, drained   1 can tomatoes salsa

Mix together use as dip. 1/2 gram per 1/2 cup.

HOT CHILI CHEESE DIP

1 (15 1/2 oz.) can kidney beans, rinsed and drained

1 (8 oz.) canned stewed tomatoes

1 T chili powder

1/8 t ground red pepper

1 1/2 c shredded no-fat cheddar cheese

Fat-free crackers

1/4 t dried oregano leaves

chopped parsley

Coarsley chop beans. In 1 quart pan combine beans, tomatoes, chili powder, oregano, andground red pepper. Cook over medium heat, stirring occasionally. Heated throughly. Stir in 3/4 cup cheese. Top with remaining cheese and parsley.

Yield 2 cups   Fat: 0 grms per serving

MOCK GUACAMOLE

2 (10 1/2 oz.) cans cut asparagus, drained

1 c finely chopped tomato

1/4 c finely chopped onion

1 T fat-free mayonnaise

1/2 t chili powder

2 T lemon juice

1/2 t garlic salt

1/4 t hot sauce

Position knife blade in food processor bowl; add asparagus. Process until smooth; transfer to a mixing bowl. Stir in tomato and remaining ingredients. Place mixture in a paper towel-lined wire-mesh strainer or colander and let drain 1 hour. Cover and chill at least 3 hours.

Yield: 2 cups   Fat: .5 grms per serving

BASIC CHEESE SAUCE DIP

2 c (1 lb.) fat free cottage cheese

2 T lemon juice

1/4 c skim milk

2 to 8 T of honey

Blend cottage cheese, lemon juice, and skim milk together until smooth. Add 2 to 4 tablespoons of honey per l cup sauce depending on taste.

Yield: 2 cups   Fat: 0 grms per serving

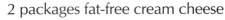

FAT-FREE CHEESE SPREAD

2 packages fat-free cream cheese

2 T chopped onion

1/4 c chopped bell pepper

1 small can crushed pineapple, drained

1 T seasoned salt

Mix together. Chill.

Fat: 0 grms per serving

FIESTA BLACKEYE PEA DIP

1 (15 oz.) can Green Giant or Joan of Arc Blackeye Peas, drained

1 (15 1/2 oz.) can white hominy, drained*

1/4 c chopped fresh cilantro or parsley

1 (4 oz.) can diced mild green chilis

1 c chopped green bell pepper

1 c chopped red onion

2 medium tomatoes, chopped

1 c mild salsa

2 garlic cloves, minced

tortilla chips

Favorite

In medium bowl, combine all ingredients, mix well. Cover and refrigerate at least 2 hours, stirring occasionally. Drain and serve with tortilla chips.

Yield: 8 cups   Fat: 1 grm per serving

*Tips: one (15 1/4 oz.) can Green Giant Whole Kernal Corn, drained, can be substituted for hominy. This recipe can also be served as a salad (try chopped celery in this).

SUPER BOWL DIP

Favorite

1 package no-fat cream cheese

1/2 envelope powdered low-fat ranch dressing

1 c picante sauce

Mix together and chill. Good dipping with no-fat chips, pretzels, or vegetables.

Fat: 1 grm total

HONEY YOGURT DIP

1 c non-fat plain yogurt

2 to 3 T honey (depending on desired sweetness)

Mix together.

Yield: 1 cup   Fat: 0 grm per serving

MARSHMALLOW CREME DIP

1 13 oz. jar marshmallow creme

1 8 oz. package fat-free Cream Cheese

1 small can or 1/4 fresh diced pineapple

Favorite

Whip together with electric mixer until light and fluffy.

Yield: approximately 2 cups   Fat: 0 grms per serving

CINNAMON POPCORN

Pop Weavers low fat microwave popcorn, or air popcorn. After popping corn, spread in oblong pan. Spray pop corn with Buttered Flavored Pam and sprinkle with Equal and cinnamon.

Fat: 2 grms per serving

CRISPY RICE AND MARSHMALLOW TREATS

4 c miniature marshmallows   4 c crispy rice cereal

1 t vanilla   1 t Molly McButter

3/4 c graham crackers, ground (12 graham cracker squares)

Place marshmallows in large saucepan, sprayed with non-stick cooking spray. Melt over low heat, removing from heat time to time to keep from burning (or use microwave to melt). Add vanilla and Molly McButter when melted. Combine mixture of cereal and crackers, add to marshmallows. Press mixture into large baking dish sprayed with non-stick spray. Allow to cool 20 to 30 minutes before cutting.

Serves 8   Fat: 1 grm per serving

APPLE ENCHILADAS

2 cans Apple Pie filling

12 fat-free flour tortillas

Sauce:

1 c sugar

1/2 T cinnamon

1 t nutmeg

1/4 c Butter Buds, liquid

Favorite

2 T cornstarch

2 1/4 c water

1/4 t salt

Place apples in tortillas and roll up like enchiladas. Place in Pam sprayed 9 x 13 pan. Make sauce, cook until thick, stir in Butter Buds. Pour over enchiladas and cover with foil. Bake at 350 degrees for 30 to 35 minutes or until warm throughout.

BAKED TURKEY EGG ROLLS

2 T soy sauce

4 c finely shredded Chinese cabbage

1 medium carrot, finely shredded (1/2 cup)

1/2 lb. ground turkey

2 t grated ginger root

1 t cornstarch

1 c bean sprouts

2 T sliced green onion

1/2 t five spice powder

1 lb. egg roll skins (14 to 16)

Mix soy sauce and cornstarch; reserve. Spray with cooking spray wok or large non-stick skillet. Heat over high heat until hot. Add cabbage, bean sprouts, carrots and onions; stir-fry 5 to 7 minutes or until cabbage is wilted. Remove from wok or skillet. Add ground turkey, five-spice powder and ginger root, stir-fry over medium heat until turkey is no longer pink. Add reserved soy sauce mixture and the cabbage mixture; cook and stir about 1 minute or until thickened. Cool turkey mixture. Place 1/4 cup turkey mixture slightly below center of egg roll skin. (Cover remaining skins with dampened towel to keep them pliable.) Fold corner of egg roll skin closest to filling over filling, tucking the point under. Fold in and overlap the 2 opposite corners. Brush fourth corner with water, roll up enclosed filling to seal. Repeat with remaining. (Cover filled egg rolls with dampened towel or plastic wrap to keep them from drying out.) Heat oven to 400 degrees. Spray cookie sheet with non-stick cooking spray. Place egg rolls, seam sides down, on cookie sheet. Lightly spray egg rolls with cooking spray. Bake 15 to 20 minutes or until golden brown.

"Call unto me, and I will answer you, and show you great and mighty things, which you know not."

Jeremiah 33:3

Soup and Sandwiches

POCKET BREAD SANDWICH

Kangaroo Fat-Free pocket bread

6 to 8 mushrooms

fat-free shredded cheese (cheddar or mozzarella)

alfalfa sprouts

stalk broccoli

tomato

Chop up mushrooms and broccoli. Sauté in Pam and put in the pocket bread. Add the alfalfa sprouts and tomatoes. Choose the cheese you like or use both. Stuff the cheese into the bread. Put into the toaster oven to melt cheese and make pocket bread crispy.

Fat: 0 grms per serving

GRILLED CHEESE SANDWICH

Spray slices of low-fat bread with butter-flavored Pam. Place fat-free cheese slices between bread. Grill in skillet.

Fat: 1 grm per serving

Deli thin ham or turkey can be used - Fat: 2 grms per serving

CHEESY PITA PIZZA

1 pita bread

Pizza toppings: (chopped green or red pepper, onion, water chestnuts, etc.)

2 T Kraft Fat-Free Italian dressing

2 Kraft Free cheese singles

Brush bread lightly with 1 tablespoon of dressing. Place on cookie sheet. Bake at 375° for 8 to 10 minutes. Brush bread with remaining dressing; top with cheese and toppings. Bake 1 to 2 minutes or when cheese begins to melt. Cut into 6 wedges.

Serves 2   Fat: 1 grm per serving

SALSA CHICKEN MELT

2 slices sourdough bread

3 oz. chicken breast

1 Kraft Free cheese single

1 T salsa

Make sandwich of cheese, salsa and chicken. Spray outsides of bread with butter flavored spray and brown in skillet.

Fat: 4 grms per serving

FAVORITE REUBEN

2 slices rye bread

1 Kraft Free cheese single

2 oz. lean turkey pastrami

1 T Kraft Fat-Free Thousand Island dressing

1/4 c sauerkraut drained

butter flavored spray

Make sandwich, spray bread with butter flavored spray and brown in skillet.

Fat: 4 grms per serving

TEMPTING TUNA MELTS

1 can (6 1/8 oz.) tuna in water, drained and flaked

1/4 c Kraft Fat-Free mayonnaise

2 English muffins, split and toasted

8 Kraft Free cheese singles

1/4 c green onions

1/4 t ground cumin

4 tomato slices

1/4 c red pepper

1/8 t black pepper

4 lettuce leaves

Favorite

Mix tuna, dressing, onions, red pepper and seasoning. Top each muffin half with lettuce, tomato, and tuna mixture. Place on cookie sheet. Broil 1 minute. Top with 2 cheese singles. Broil 1 minute or until cheese melts.

Makes 4 sandwiches   Fat: 2 grms per serving

FAT-FREE CREAM SOUP

1 c non-fat dried milk powder

2 T cornstarch

2 T chicken bouillon powder

1/4 t black pepper

1 T dried onion flakes

1/2 t dried basil

1/2 t dried thyme

Mix all ingredients and store in airtight container. To make soup base, add 2 cups cold water to the mix in a large saucepan and stir constantly over medium heat until thick. You can use this base to make any flavor "cream" soup; just add your main ingredient to the mix (mushrooms, for example) and cook a few minutes longer. If the soup is too thick, add more water and stir thoroughly over medium heat.

Approximately 4 to 6 cups (varies upon additions)

HOMEMADE POTATO SOUP

4 small raw potatoes

1/2 c chopped onion

1/4 c celery, chopped

1/2 t butter flavor

Favorite

2 c chicken broth

1/4 c green pepper, chopped

1 T flour

1/4 c skim milk

Combine all ingredients and cook until tender.

Serves 4   Fat: 0 grms per serving

CHICKEN NOODLE SOUP

4 oz. skinless, diced, and cooked chicken breast

8 c chicken broth, defatted

Linguini noodles

carrots, diced

celery, diced

Bring broth to boil in a 3 quart pan. Add vegetables, reduce heat, and simmer until tender. Add chicken and noodles. Simmer until noodles are cooked and tender. Add salt and pepper to taste.

Fat: 8 grms total

Hint: You can use the broth off your chicken if you put the broth in freezer for awhile then remove any fat on top.

HOMEMADE VEGETABLE SOUP

3 c low-sodium beef broth

2 c low-salt V-8

2 medium potatoes

1/4 t pepper

2 c green beans

2 c tomatoes, chopped

3 sliced carrots

2 stalks celery, chopped

1/4 c green pepper, chopped

2 t dried parsley flakes

1/4 c skim milk

1 medium onion, chopped

Combine broth, V-8, tomatoes, onions, carrots, celery, green pepper, and potatoes. Combine all ingredients and cook until tender.

Serves 4   Fat: 0 grms per serving

HEARTY CHICKEN VEGETABLE SOUP

2 c fresh green beans

2 T lemon juice

1 (16 oz.) can tomatoes

1/4 t pepper

1 1/2 c chicken breast, cubed

2 T chopped fresh parlsey

1 onion, chopped

6 carrots, chopped

2 stalks celery, diced

1/4 head cabbage, chopped

1 c cooked rice or pasta

8 c chicken broth, de-fatted

Steam green beans with lemon juice until tender. Combine tomatoes, onions, carrots, celery, and pepper in stock pot with chicken broth and slowly bring to a boil. Reduce heat and simmer 1-2 hours or until vegetables are tender. Add beans and cabbage, simmer 15 minutes. Add chicken and rice or pasta; heat. Sprinkle with parsley.

Serves 10-12   Fat: 1 grm per serving

NANCY'S LOW-FAT REUBEN SANDWICH

Fat-free Swiss cheese

1 T Fat-free cold slaw

Rye bread

Mustard

Your choice: turkey or turkey pastrami

Make cold slaw with fat-free**Favorite** Mayo or use prepared fat-free cold slaw dressing. Put all items between bread, spray bread with butter flavored Pam and grill. This would also be good in pocket bread!

TACO SOUP

4 chicken breasts

1 1/2 t salt

1 1/2 oz. pkg. taco seasoning mix

1 (4 oz.) can green chilis, chopped

1 can kidney or great northern beans

1 1/2 c or more of water or de-fatted chicken broth

1 c onion, chopped

1/2 t pepper

1 can hominy

1 can pinto beans

3 pints canned tomatoes

Favorite

Cook in crockpot overnight or boil chicken until done. Chop in food processor as fine as you like. Mix into chicken dry ingredients. Add vegetables, and water (or defatted broth). Bring to low boil, cover and simmer 30 or 40 minutes or put in crock pot and forget it. Two cups of cooked pintos can be used instead of canned ones.

Makes about one gallon.

*Note: There is 12 grams of fat in the chicken breasts-so there is 12 grams in the gallon of soup.

LEMON-PEPPER ASPARAGUS SOUP

1/2 c chicken broth, de-fatted

1 pkg. (10 oz.) frozen cut asparagus

1/2 c instant mashed potato flakes

1 T lemon juice

1/8 t cracked black pepper

1 T finely snipped parsley

In a 2-quart saucepan, bring the broth and asparagus to a boil, then reduce the heat. Simmer for 3 minutes. Stir in the potato flakes, lemon juice, and pepper. Cover and simmer until the asparagus is just tender, 1 to 2 minutes. Stir in parsley.

Serves 4   Low Fat: 1.2 grms per serving

SKINNY VEGGIE SANDWICH

For best flavor, use chilled ingredients

Low fat bread

Fat-free mayo

Season all salt

Thinly sliced: purple onion, fresh mushroom, cucumbers, and golden apples

Spread mayo on chilled bread. Alternate layers of season salt and the different veggies. Wrap in plastic wrap and eat later or chow down immediately. This is a great summer sandwich, cool and refreshing. Best of all, the only fat is in the bread. It would be good in a pita pocket!

S O U P & SANDWICHES

TENNIE'S' QUICK STOUP

Stoup - That's what I call a concoction that's not quite stew or soup!

2 cans of stewed tomatoes

1/2 to 3/4 c Minute Rice

1 can fat-free chicken broth

Favorite

1 can pinto beans with jalapeno

1 cooked chicken breast, chopped

Season to taste with: chili powder, onion powder, garlic powder and salt.

Add tomatoes and chicken broth together, bring to a boil. Add Minute Rice, cover and lower heat for 5 minutes. Add seasonings, chicken and beans. Continue on low heat 15 or 20 minutes. Look out, get back Jack!!! It is great. Serve with fat-free shredded cheese on top. Good with fat-free crackers or fat-free cornbread!

COWBOY STEW

1 can Ranch Style Beans

1 can Rotel tomatoes

2-3 t chili powders

Favorite

1 can corn

1 can whole tomatoes

2-3 chopped potatoes

Do not drain the canned vegetables. Mix all ingredients together, simmer a couple of hours.

FRENCH ONION SOUP

3 beef bouillon cubes

1/2 t Worcestershire sauce

2 qt. water

1 chicken bouillon cube

4 to 5 slices onion

salt and pepper to taste

Cook until tender. Toast bread slices, let set out till they get hard. Melt fat-free Swiss cheese on bread and float on top of soup.

"… diligence is a man's most precious possession."
Proverbs 12:27

Salads and Dressings

MEXICAN RICE SALAD

8 oz. Ranch non-fat dressing

1 t chili powder

2 c cooked rice

1/4 c sliced green onions

1 c fat-free shredded cheddar cheese

10 oz. frozen corn, thawed and drained

Favorite

2 t chopped jalapeños

1 chopped red pepper

1 can black beans

Mix non-fat dressing, jalapeño peppers, and chili powder in large bowl. Add remaining ingredients, mix lightly and refrigerate.

Serves 4   Fat: 1 grm per serving

CORN SALAD

1 can Mexicorn (drained)

Kraft Fat-Free Ranch dressing

1 chopped green onion

Mix together.

Serves 4   Fat: 0 grms per serving

SUMMER RICE SALAD

Salad:

4 c cooked rice

1/2 red chopped sweet pepper

1/2 chopped green sweet pepper

1 c canned corn, drained

1 c water packed artichokes, drained

2 chopped green onions

1/2 t salt

2 stalks chopped celery

Dressing:

1 c fat-free Italian dressing

1 1/2 t dry Ranch dressing mix

2 T chopped onion

In large bowl, combine all ingredients for salad. Set aside. Place all ingredients for dressing in food processor or blender and mix until onion is pureed. Pour over salad and toss. Chill for 2 to 3 hours before serving.

Serves 8   Fat: 0 grms per serving

PASTA SALAD

1 lb. grilled chicken, chopped

4 chicken bouillon cubes

1 8 oz. bottle honey dijon fat-free dressing

1 cup chopped green bell pepper

1 med. chopped purple onion

1 (15 oz.) can red kidney beans, drained

1 (8 oz.) pkg. elbow macaroni

Pam spray

Cook macaroni according to package directions, adding bouillon cubes to water. Partially thaw chicken and cut into bite size pieces. Spray Pam in a heavy pan and sear chicken. Drain macaroni and return to pan. Pour on dressing. Add chicken, bell pepper, onion, and beans. Mix thoroughly. Good warm or cold.

Serves 4   Fat: 3 grms per serving

DINNER SALAD

3 c torn greens (Romaine, Boston, Bibb, or leaf)

1 c sliced mushrooms

1/2 c fat-free herb dressing

2 hard-boiled eggs (white only)

In large bowl, combine lettuce and mushrooms. Pour dressing over vegetables and toss to coat. Sprinkle evenly with egg whites.

Serves 8   Fat: 0 grms per serving

CURRY RICE SALAD

1 1/2 c cooked rice

3/4 t curry powder

1/4 c minced onion

Refrigerate 3 hours. Add: 1 cup chopped celery, 1 can drained green peas or uncooked frozen peas, 1 small can partially drained pineapple Tidbits.

Combine: 3/4 c no-fat mayonnaise, 1 T vinegar, 1 t canola oil, (optional) mix well into rest of ingredients. Stir into chilled rice. Extra pineapple juice may be added if it gets dry.

SPINACH-ORANGE SALAD

Raspberry vinaigrette

2 T raspberry vinegar

1/4 c orange juice

1/4 t salt

4 thin sliced red onion rings

1 lb. fresh spinach, or greens (2 cups), trimmed & rinsed

2 Naval oranges, peeled & sliced

Make raspberry vinaigrette; combine all ingredients in small jar with tight fitting lid; shake well.

Divide spinach, orange, and onion evenly over 4 chilled plates. Drizzle vinaigrette over each.

Serves 4   Fat: 0 grms per serving

RANCH POTATO SALAD

1 oz. low-fat Hidden Valley Ranch dressing mix   1/2 c chopped red onion

8 medium Russet potatoes (boiled, peeled, and cubed)   1/4 c water

1 c sliced celery

1/2 c fat-free mayonnaise

Combine potatoes, celery, and onion. Combine Ranch dressing, mayonnaise, and water; add to potato mixture and toss to coat. Chill.

Serves 4 to 6   Fat: 1 grm per serving (4 servings)

SIN-FREE COLESLAW

2 c shredded cabbage   2 T cider vinegar

1 c shredded carrots   1 T lemon juice

1/2 c slivered bell peppers   1 T sugar

1/2 c fat-free mayonnaise   1 t celery seed

In a medium bowl, combine cabbage, carrots, peppers. In a small bowl, combine remaining ingredients. Pour dressing over slaw and toss. Chill for at least 2 hours.

Serves 6   Fat: 0 grms per serving

CHICKEN SALAD

2 c diced boneless white chicken (fat: 8 grms)   1/2 c fat-free mayonnaise

1 c chopped celery

1 (20 oz.) can pineapple chunks (save juice)

1 pkg. Kraft Fat-Free Ranch dressing mixed with 1/4 cup juice.

Toss all together and chill.

Serves 4   Fat: 2 grms per serving

RANCH CHICKEN SALAD

2 c cubed, cooked chicken   1 c sliced celery

1 can (20 oz.) pineapple chunks   1/4 c pineapple juice

1 pkg. (1 oz.) Hidden Valley Ranch Low-Fat Original Ranch salad dressing Mix

1/2 c fat-free mayonnaise

Combine chicken, celery, pineapple chunks. Separately, combine Ranch dressing, mayonnaise, and pineapple juice. Add to chicken mixture and toss well. Chill.

Serves 4 to 6   Fat: 6 grms for 4 servings

CRAB SALAD

1/2 lb crabmeat   4 c diced celery

1 c diced onion   1/4 c diced bell pepper

1 1/2 t salt   1 1/2 c fat-free mayonnaise

Mix, chill, and serve over lettuce leaf.

Serves 2   Fat: 1 grm per serving

EASY PASTA

1 lb. favorite pasta

1/2 c fat-free Italian dressing

1 lb. frozen broccoli

Cook pasta in boiling water. Steam broccoli in Italian dressing. Combine both. Serve hot or cold; substitute vegetables or a combination.

Serves 4   Fat: 1 grm per serving

DELICIOUS FRUIT SALAD

1/2 can of #2 sliced peaches

1/2 c marachino cherries, halved

2 reg. pkg. instant vanilla pudding

2 (15 1/4 oz.) cans pineapple chunks, in own juice

3 bananas sliced

Drain canned fruit and preserve juice. Combine all fruits, add a portion of reserved juice to pudding mix, stir, and add remaining fruit juice. (Caution: it will lump if mixed all at one time.) Pour over fruit. For best flavor, chill for several hours or overnight.

Serves 6   Fat: 0 grms per serving

MANDARIN ORANGE SALAD

1 (11 oz.) can Mandarin oranges, drained

1 c pineapple tidbits, save juice

1 T fat-free sour cream

1 c red seedless grapes

1 T sugar

1 c green seedless grapes

In large bowl, combine fruit. In small bowl combine juice from pineapple, sour cream and sugar. Stir until sugar is dissolved. Pour this mixture over fruit and chill 1 hour.

Serves 6   Fat: 0 grms per serving

CREAMY FRUIT SALAD

1 c prepared Dream Whip

1 (8 oz.) can pineapple tidbits, drained

1 (8 oz.) jar cherries, drained

3 bananas, sliced

1 c fat-free sour cream

1/2 c sugar

1/2 c Grape Nuts (optional)

Favorite

Combine all ingredients and blend well. Chill 30 minutes.

Serves 12   Fat: 0 grms per serving

MELANIE'S CUCUMBER AND ONION SALAD

4 medium cucumbers, thinly sliced

Salt

1 c vinegar

2 red onions, thinly sliced

1 c water

4 T sugar

Favorite

In a 2 quart casserole, layer cucumbers and onions, sprinkle with salt. Repeat layers and salt. Cover tightly and drain off liquid every hour for three hours. Combine water, vinegar and sugar and pour over cucumber mixture. Cover and refrigerate overnight.

SALLY'S PASTA SALAD

1 package No-Yoke Noodles

Onions, Bell Peppers, Celery, Tomatoes

Favorite

Fat-free Italian dressing

Dry Ranch dressing

Cook and drain noodles. Add Italian dressing, mix well and refrigerate. Chop vegetables, add to noodles and sprinkle with dry ranch dressing. Add more Italian dressing if it seems dry.

WALDORF ORANGE SALAD

1/4 c orange juice

1/2 c fat-free mayonnaise

2 T honey

1 c Mandarin orange sections, drained

1 c chopped apples

1/3 c raisins

1/2 head shredded lettuce

In a medium bowl, combine juice, mayonnaise, and honey. Blend well. Add orange sections, apples, and raisins. Chill for 1 hour. Serve on 1 cup shredded lettuce.

Serves 3   Fat: 0 grms per serving

FRESH FRUIT SALAD WITH POPPY SEED DRESSING

1 small pineapple

1 c. green grapes

1 c red grapes

2 c sliced strawberries

1 recipe "Poppy Seed Dressing"

2 c honeydew melon

2 c cantalope

2 c watermelon

1 peach

lemon juice

Cut fruit into chunks. Squeeze lemon juice over fruit; toss together in a large bowl. Chill and serve with poppy seed dressing, if desired.

Serves 6   Fat: 0 grms per serving

FAT-FREE POPPY SEED DRESSING

1 t unflavored gelatin

1 t dry apricot Jell-O

1 t onion juice

1 T poppy seeds

2 c unsweetened pineapple juice

Favorite

2 1/2 T honey

1/2 t dry mustard

dash of lime juice

dash of salt (optional)

Place gelatin, Jell-O and pineapple juice in saucepan; let stand 1 minute. Cook over medium heat, stirring constantly; 2 to 3 minutes until dissolved. Whisk in remaining ingredients and chill at least 5 hours. Serve over fresh fruit.

Yields: 2 1/4 cups or 36 T   Fat: 0 grms per serving

SALAD DRESSING OR DIP

1 c Miracle Whip Free

Juice of Mandarin oranges*

2 T vinegar

1-2 pkgs. artificial sweetener

Poppy seeds (or any type of seasoning)

Mix together, adding enough juice,thin to desired consistency.

* Pineapple juice or fresh juice from oranges is good also. You might try using the mandarin oranges in your salad.

HONEY MUSTARD DRESSING

1 1/4 c fat-free mayonnaise

1/4 c yellow mustard

1/4 t cayenne pepper, optional

1 t minced garlic

Favorite

1/4 c honey

1/3 c apple cider vinegar

1/2 c water

Place all ingredients in a bowl and blend together.

Yields: 2 1/2 cups   Fat: 0 grms per serving

ROSY ITALIAN DRESSING

1/2 c + 1 T non-fat buttermilk

1/4 c + 1 T non-fat mayonnaise

1/4 t dried oregano

1/4 t pepper

1 clove garlic crushed

1/4 c tomato juice

1 T grated onion

1/4 t dried basil

1/4 t paprika

Combine all ingredients in a small bowl, stirring well with a small whisk. Cover and chill.

Yield: 1 cup + 2 T   Fat: 0 grms per serving

"And Jesus said to them, 'I am the bread of life. He who comes to Me shall never hunger, and he who believes in Me shall never thirst.' "

John 6:35

Bread, Stuffings, and Rice Dishes

"GOOD STUFF, MAYNARD"

1 pkg. yeast

1/2 c sugar

2 1/2 c flour

1/2 c warm water

cinnamon & sugar sprinkle

l c warm water

dash of salt

1 pkg. Butter Buds

1/2 c brown sugar

Dissolve yeast in l cup warm water. Mix in 1/2 cup sugar and salt. Mix in flour. Let rise till double in size. Mix 1 package Butter Buds, brown sugar and 1/2 cup warm water. Spray tube pan with non-stick spray. Pour Butter Buds mixture in bottom of tube pan. After bread has risen, punch down. Divide into small pieces and place in pan. (Makes two layers.) Sprinkle top with cinnamon and sugar, let rise again. Bake in 350° oven till done, or brown on top. Turn tube pan upside down on a cake plate while still hot. Let cool and slice. Refrigerate. Very good for breakfast.

Serves 8   Fat: 0.5 grms per serving

FAT FREE CORNBREAD

1 c cornmeal

1 t salt

1 c skim milk

1/4 c non-fat yogurt

Favorite

1/2 c flour

3 t baking powder

2 egg whites

Spray iron skillet with Pam and heat skillet in oven. Mix ingredients, pour into skillet and bake at 400° for 17 minutes.

Fat per serving: Low Fat: 0 grms

EASY HOT ROLLS

1 c warm water

4 T sugar

Favorite

1 pkg. yeast

2 1/2 c flour

Mix warm water and yeast. Add dash of salt. Mix in other ingredients. Let rise to double. Then make rolls. Place in muffin pan and let rise again. Bake at 425° until brown.

Fat: .5 grms per serving

RANCH BREAD

French bread   Butter-Flavored Pam

Low-fat Hidden Valley Ranch original Ranch salad dressing mix

Spray slices of French bread with Pam and sprinkle with Ranch dressing mix. Broil until toasted.

Fat: 2-3 grms per serving

GARLIC-CHEESE HOME-STYLE BISCUITS

2 c Pioneer low-fat biscuit mix

3/4 c + 1 T evaporated skim milk

1/2 c fat-free grated cheddar cheese

garlic salt to taste

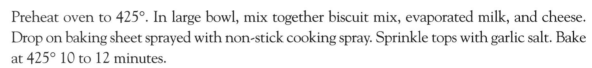

Preheat oven to 425°. In large bowl, mix together biscuit mix, evaporated milk, and cheese. Drop on baking sheet sprayed with non-stick cooking spray. Sprinkle tops with garlic salt. Bake at 425° 10 to 12 minutes.

Fat: .5 grms per serving

DINNER ROLLS

2 pkg. dry yeast   2 c warm water

1/2 c sugar   1 1/2 t salt

2 Egg Beaters   5 c bread flour

1/4 c Butter Buds, liquid

Dissolve yeast in warm water in large bowl. Add sugar, salt, Egg Beaters, Butter Buds, and one cup of flour. Beat until smooth. Stir in rest of the flour and continue stirring until smooth. Cover and let rise in a warm place until it doubles in size (about 30 or 40 minutes). Spoon batter into 24 muffin cups sprayed with a non-fat cooking spray. Fill each cup about 1/2 full. Let rise until dough reaches the top of the muffin tins (20 to 30 minutes). Bake at 400° for 12-15 minutes.

Serves 24   Fat per serving: Low Fat: .4 grms, Regular Fat: 2.17 grms

Regular margarine: Fat: 11.5 grms per tablespoon

BREAD CRUMBS

6 slices Wonder Light reduced calorie fat-free bread
Butter flavored Pam no-stick cooking spray

Spray both sides of each bread slice with Pam and bake in a 250° oven until toasted. Turn slices over and toast until brown and dry. Crumb bread in food processor. Store in air-tight container in freezer and use as needed.

Makes 3 cups   Fat: 0 grms per serving

BANANA NUT BREAD

3/4 c egg beaters
1/2 c sugar
1 3/4 c flour
1 t baking powder

1/2 t soda
1/2 t salt
2 mashed bananas
1 t butter flavoring

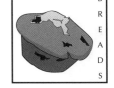

Combine all ingredients, pour into greased loaf pan, bake at 375° for 30 to 40 minutes or until toothpick comes out clean.

Serves 6   Fat: .5 grms per serving

BETTY'S APRICOT BREAD

2 1/2 c flour
1/2 c sugar
1 pkg. yeast

Favorite

1 c warm water
1 t salt
2 c chopped dried apricots*

Mix water, fruit, sugar, salt, and yeast in blender or bowl. Stir in flour and let rise until double. Punch down with spoon. Dump in loaf pan sprayed with Pam. Let rise again, then cook at 350° until brown.

*Any dried fruit may be used. This recipe will also adapt to bread makers very well.

Fat: 0.5 grms per serving

CARROT MUFFINS

2 1/4 c flour	1/2 c sugar
1 t cinnamon	1 t salt
1 t baking soda	1/2 t baking powder
1/4 t ginger	1 T powder sugar
1 8 oz. vanilla no-fat yogurt	1/2 c egg beaters
1/2 c unsweetened applesauce	1/2 c raisins
3 med. finely shredded carrots	1/3 c brown sugar
1 t vanilla	

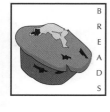

Preheat oven to 350°. Spray muffin pan with Pam. Combine flour, sugar, cinnamon, salt, baking soda, baking powder, and ginger. In separate bowl, mix carrots, yogurt, egg beaters, applesauce, raisins, brown sugar, and vanilla with wire wisk until well blended. With spoon, stir in flour mixture until flour is moistened. Spoon batter into muffin pans. Bake 30 minutes or until toothpick inserted in middle of muffin comes out clean. Sprinkle with powdered sugar.

Serves 8   Fat: 0 grms per serving

OLD FASHION CORNBREAD DRESSING

1 1/2 c chopped onion	1 1/2 c chopped celery
1/2 c Butter Buds	1 t poultry seasoning
1 t sage	1 t salt
3 Egg Beaters	
1 1/2 c defatted chicken broth	
fat-free cornbread recipe	
white bread (1 grm fat) or fat-free biscuits	

Cook and stir onions and celery in Butter Buds over medium heat until tender. Stir in seasonings. Add onion mixture, egg beaters, and broth to cornbread and bread in large bowl. Cook in 350° oven until desired doneness.

Serves 4   Low Fat: 2 grms per serving, Reg Fat: 14.25 grms per serving

SAVORY CRANBERRY STUFFING

1 c chopped celery

1 c chopped onion

1/2 c Butter Buds liquid

1 (16 oz.) can whole berry cranberry sauce

2 T chicken instant bouillon or 6 cubes

16 slices dry bread (12 c bread cubes) low-fat (.05 grms per slice)

1 c grape nuts

2 t poultry seasoning

1 t sage

3 c hot water

Cook celery and onions in Butter Buds liquid until tender. In small sauce pan, over low heat, stir in cranberry sauce and bouillon until bouillon dissolves. In large bowl, combine remaining ingredients; add celery and cranberry mixtures. Mix well, Place in greased baking dish, Bake at 350° for 30 minutes or stuff turkey.

Serves 4   Fat: 4 grms per serving

ZUCCHINI SQUASH DRESSING

1 medium pan fat-free cornbread

6 small zucchini squash, peeled and grated

1 c chopped onion

1 c chopped celery

1 c chopped bell pepper

2 c skim milk

1 can low-fat cream of chicken soup

2 Egg Beaters or 2 egg whites

salt and pepper to taste

poultry seasoning

Favorite

Crumble fat-free cornbread, add 2 cups milk. Soak. Add vegetables, cream of chicken soup, salt and pepper and poultry seasoning to taste. Add 2 Egg Beaters. Mix all and bake 30 minutes at 375°.

Fat: 2 grms per serving

CAJUN-STYLE RED BEANS AND BROWN RICE

1 lb. dried pinto beans

1 c chopped green onion

1/2 t minced garlic

3/4 t pepper

1/4 t oregano

1 t Worcestershire sauce

6 oz. tomato paste

1 t celery flakes

2 c chopped yellow onion

1 c chopped green bell pepper

1/4 t red cayenne pepper

1/2 t salt

1/4 t garlic powder

3 dashes tabasco sauce

1/4 t thyme

6 cups cooked brown rice

Favorite

Wash beans and soak for 12 hours. Drain water. In a large pot, add water to 1/2" above beans level. Add remaining ingredients, except rice; cook covered over low heat 2 to 2 1/2 hours. Serve over cooked brown rice.

Fat:1.3 grms per serving

B
R
E
A
D
S

WILD RICE MEDLEY

4 oz. wild rice (or brown rice)

4 oz. enriched converted rice

8 sliced scallions

To prepare wild rice, wash grains thoroughly. Place in a heavy 2-quart saucepan with 4 cups salted water. Bring to a boil, cover and reduce heat. Simmer about 45 minutes or until rice is tender but not mushy. All water may not be absorbed. Remove cover, fluff rice with a fork, and simmer about 5 minutes more; drain any excess liquid. Meanwhile, cook white rice according to package directions so that it will be ready at about the same time as the wild rice. Combine both kinds of rice in serving bowl and stir in scallions. Serve at once.

Serves 8   Fat: 2 grms per serving

CREOLE RICE

1 c Uncle Bens Rice

1/2 of a large onion

1/2 of a large bell pepper

1 can Mushrooms

4 t Accent

2 cans consommé, add water (heat)

1/4 stick no-fat margarine

1 jar pimentos

1 can low-fat Mushroom soup

Brown rice in Pam. Add chopped onions and bell peppers. Cook a few minutes. Pour into casserole, add rest of ingredients. Add heated consommé. Cover-Bake 3-4 hours at 275°.

ORIENTAL FRIED RICE

1 1/4 c chicken broth, defatted

2 T light soy sauce

1/2 t ground ginger

1 1/2 c minute brown rice

2 c (1/2 pkg.) frozen broccoli, red pepper, bamboo shoots, and mushrooms

1/8 t garlic powder

1 T cornstarch

Bring broth, soy sauce, ginger, garlic powder to a boil. Stir in rice, bring to a boil to thicken. Reduce heat, cover, and simmer for 5 minutes. Mix cornstarch with warm water. Add to rice along with vegetables. Bring to a boil to thicken. Remove from heat and let stand 5 minutes.

Serves 4   Fat: 1 grm per serving

HERBED RICE PILAF

1 c uncooked long grain rice

1 c chopped celery

3/4 c chopped onion

Pam

1/4 c fat free margarine

2 1/2 c water

1 package dry chicken noodle soup mix

2 T minced parsley

1/2 t dried thyme

1/4 t sage

1/4 t pepper

1 T chopped pimientos

In a large skillet, cook rice, celery, and onion in Pam; stirring constantly, brown rice. Add all remaining ingredients except pimientos. Reduce heat; cover and simmer for 15 minutes. Stir in pimientos. Remove from heat and let stand; covered for 10 minutes.

WHOLE-WHEAT PIZZA CRUST

2 c all-purpose flour

1 c whole-wheat flour

1 package dry yeast

1 c warm water

2 t cornmeal

To make the crust.

Stir together 1 cup of the all-purpose flour with 1/4 cup of the whole-wheat flour and the yeast. Add the warm water. Beat with an electric mixer on low speed for 30 seconds. Scrape the bowl. Then beat on high speed for 3 minutes. With a spoon, stir in the remaining 3/4 cup of whole-wheat flour, then add as much of the remaining all-purpose flour as you can. Turn out on floured board and knead more flour in until dough is moderately stiff, smooth and elastic (about 8 minutes). Divide dough in half and let rest 10 minutes.

Prepare two 12 pizza pans. Spray with Pam and sprinkle with cornmeal. Roll out both dough mixtures and transfer to pizza pans. Bake at 425° fo 12 minutes. Do not let rise.

VEGETABLE PIZZA TOPPINGS

1 c pizza or spaghetti sauce

3 c shredded fat-free mozzarella, and or cheddar cheese

1 c each chopped red and green bell pepper

1 c sliced mushrooms

1/2 c onions

To make topping: Spread the sauce on top of crust. Sprinkle on vegetables and cover with cheese. Bake for 10 to 15 minutes more or until cheese is bubbly.

*"Better is a dinner of herbs where love is
than a fatted calf with hatred."*
Proverbs 15:17

Meat
and
Fish

CHILI PASTA GRANDE

1 pickled chopped jalapeño pepper

1 can Italian-style tomatoes

1/2 c fat-free sour cream

2 t chili powder

4 oz. (about one cup) elbow macaroni, cooked and drained

1 onion, chopped

1 can kidney beans, drained

chopped cilantro (optional)

1/4 t ground cumin

Favorite

Spray large skillet with cooking spray. Heat over medium heat. Add onion, cook, stirring constantly, 2 minutes. Add undrained tomatoes, kidney beans, jalapeño pepper, chili powder, and cumin. Bring to a boil. Reduce heat and simmer, stirring occasionally, 15 minutes. Toss with macaroni. Serve with sour cream and cilantro.

Serves 4   Fat: 1 grm per serving

LITE MEATBALLS

1 lb. super lean ground beef

scant 1/4 c Egg Beaters

1 scant T. minced onion

2 slices fat-free bread

1 chicken bouillon cube dissolved in 1/2 c boiling water

Pam

1/4 c dry oatmeal

1 T dried parsley

1 t Worcestershire

1/2 c ketchup

Combine all ingredients except ketchup mixing well. Form into balls and place on a cookie sheet that has been coated with Pam. Cover with foil and bake about 5 minutes at 350°. Uncover, dot each meatball with ketchup and bake uncovered about 10 more minutes. Do not over bake.

Makes 50   Fat: .33 grms per serving

HAMBURGERS

3 oz. extra lean hamburger meat

1 t each chopped broccoli, cauliflower, onion, green pepper, and cooked rice

1 t fat-free yogurt

dash sasoned pepper

1 low-fat hamburger bun

1 grm. fat-free American cheese

Mix (chopped or in food processor) broccoli, cauliflower, onion, green pepper, cooked rice, non-fat yogurt, and seasoned pepper to taste. (Any vegetable or non-fat crackers or filler can be used to increase the portion of patty) Add to hamburger and make patty. One patty: 6 grms of fat. Low fat hamburger bun: 1 grm.

Fat: 7 grms per hamburger

BEEF NOODLE SUPPER

1 lb. lean ground beef, cooked, drained, and rinsed

1/2 c (2 oz.) grated fat-free mozzarella cheese.

1/2 c onion

1/2 c bell pepper

1 (12 oz.) can V-8 juice

2 c cooked drained noodles

Place cooked beef, onion, and green pepper in a large skillet sprayed with Pam. Sauté quickly 1-2 minutes, add V-8 juice and simmer 5 minutes. Mix beef with noodles, place in sprayed casserole, and bake 15 minutes at 350°. Sprinkle with cheese and bake until cheese melts.

Serves 6   Fat: 3 grms per serving

RANCH STEAK

1/2 of a 2 oz. pkg. of Hidden Valley Ranch Low Fat Dressing Mix

1 lb. top sirloin steak

3 T. Water

1 envelope Butter Buds, dry

Grill sirloin for 4 minutes. Mix water, Ranch mix and Butter Buds together to make a paste. Brush steak with 1/2 of the mixture. Grill 3 minutes longer. Turn and grill 4 minutes. Brush on remaining mixture and grill 3 to 5 minutes more.

Serves 4   Fat: 10.1 grms per 4 oz. serving

CROCK POT STEAK

1 1/2 lbs. top round steak, cut into serving pieces

1 can Campbell's Healthly Request cream of mushroom soup

1 medium can whole peeled tomatoes

1/2 t salt (optional)

1/2 t pepper

1/2 t garlic powder

1 T Worcestershire sauce

Place meat in bottom of Pam-sprayed crock pot and sprinkle with seasonings. Add soup, tomatoes, and Worcestershire. Cover and cook on low for about 3 to 4 hours. Serve over rice.

Serves 8   Fat: 5.34 grms per serving

RANCH BURGERS

1/2 of a 2 oz. pkg. of Hidden Valley Ranch Low-Fat Original Ranch salad dressing mix

1 lb. extra lean ground beef

Form into 4 patties and grill or broil until done.

Serves 4   Fat: 7 grms per serving

HAMBURGER STEAK

ONE PATTY:

3 oz. lean hamburger meat (6 grms fat)

1 egg white

1 t non-fat yogurt

1 t very finely chopped onion

1 t very finely chopped bell pepper

1/8 t seasoned pepper

2 T rice, non-fat cracker crumbs or potato flakes

sprinkle au jus gravy mix, dry

1/4 c chopped onion (I use green onions - greens and all)

1/4 c chopped bell peppers

1/4 c chopped celery

1/4 c carrots (or any other vegetables you like)

1 t Butter Buds

1/4 t au jus gravy mix, dry

1/c beef broth

1/4 c dryed mushrooms or plain, water packed

Mix first 8 ingredients together and form a patty. Set aside. Spray skillet with Pam. Brown onions, peppers, celery, and carrots. Remove vegetables. Spray skillet again with Pam. Brown one side of hamburger patty in skillet using medium heat. Spray meat with Pam before turning meat over to brown on other side. Lower heat to simmer. Add vegetables and 1/8 cup of water. Cover and simmer for about 6 minutes (checking often and adding more water as needed). This will make the meat tender and juicy but cooked.

GRAVY: Remove meat, leave some onion and peppers in skillet. Add 1/4 cup mushrooms and 1/2 cup beef broth. Mix paste of corn starch, au jus gravy mix, Butter Buds, 2 tablespoons water to thicken gravy. (Can use flour.) Serve over cooked brown or white rice or toasted low-fat or fat-free bread.

Serves 1   Fat: 7 grms per serving

CORN AND HAM BAKE

6 slices light ham cut in pieces

1/2 c fat-free shredded cheese

3 c whole kernal corn, drained

Pepper, to taste

1 c skim milk

1 1/2 T flour

1/2 t dry onion flakes

Preheat oven 350°. Mix flour and milk until smooth using a blender or food processor. Add onion and mix. Combine corn and ham in sprayed 9" square dish. Pour milk mixture over corn and ham. Season with pepper and top with shredded cheese, bake for 30 to 35 minutes.

Serves 6   Fat: 1 grm per serving

HAMBURGER, CHICKEN, OR TUNA CASSEROLE

8 oz. elbow macaroni cooked

one of the following:

1 lb. extra lean hamburger meat, cooked

2 10 oz. cans white chicken chunks in water

1 12 oz. can light chunk tuna in spring water

1/2 c chopped onion

1/2 c celery

1 16 oz. can drained corn

1 16 oz. can drained green peas

1/2 c chopped dry mushrooms

1 can Campbell's Healthy Request cream of celery soup (and/or 1 can Campbell's Healthy Request cream of mushroom soup)

1 soup can skim milk

1/2 c non-fat yogurt

1/2 packet Butter Buds

Fat-free American or cheddar cheese

1 c crushed corn flakes

To increase moisture of casserole, add 1 cup defatted beef broth with hamburger, 1 cup defatted chicken broth with the chicken or 1 cup vetegable stock with the tuna. (I use vegetable with tuna because I don't like the chicken taste with tuna). Brown onions and celery in sauce pan with Pam spray. Combine all ingredients except for cheese and corn flakes in large casserole dish. Top with cheese and corn flakes. Bake in 350° oven for 15 to 20 minutes.

Serves 8   Fat per serving: Hamburger 5 grms; Tuna 2 grms; Chicken 2 grms

SALMON PATTIES

1 (1 lb.) can pink salmon

4 egg whites

2/3 c oat bran cereal

1 medium onion finely chopped

1 T finely chopped parsley

1 T fresh lemon juice

Pam

Mix all ingredients; form into patties. Coat skillet with Pam and fry until crisp. Great with mashed potatoes and a dash of ketchup.

Serves 8   Fat: 2.8 grms per serving

BROILED HALIBUT FILETS

2 Halibut filets   4 T no-fat sour cream

1 1/2 t. dry Ranch dressing mix   2 t lemon juice

In a small bowl combine sour cream, lemon juice, and ranch dressing mix. Stir until blended. Place halibut on pan for broiling. Cover each filet with sour cream sauce. Broil 8-10 minutes. Fish is done when it flakes with a fork.

Serves 2   Fat: 2 grms per servings

TUNA AND NOODLE BAKE

1 6 oz. can of water packed tuna   2 c cooked no-yolk noodles

1 medium onion chopped   1 1/2 c chopped celery

1 can defatted chicken broth   2 t cornstarch

1 bagel, chopped small pieces   Salt and pepper

1/2 c fat-free shredded cheese

Preheat oven to 350°. Combine all ingredients in a large bowl except the bagel. Mix well. Spray medium size casserole dish with non-stick cooking spray. Pour in mixture. Sprinkle top with fat-free cheese and add chopped pieces of bagel. Bake for 30 - 40 minutes

Serves 4   Fat: 1 grm per serving

MARINATED SHRIMP

Seasoned water for boiling:

1 lb. fresh shrimp, peeled and cleaned

2 t dry celery flakes

1 T pickling spice

2 t dry onion flakes

8 c water

Marinade:

1 c fat-free Italian dressing

1/2 t celery seed

2 dashes tabasco sauce

1 medium onion, sliced

2 t green pepper flakes

Cook peeled and cleaned shrimp in 8 cups boiling water with seasonings listed above. Prepare ingredients for marinade and mix. Remove shrimp from seasoned water and arrange in shallow dish. Pour marinade over shrimp. Chill for several hours or overnight before serving.

Serves 6   Fat: 1 grm per serving

TUNA PATTIES

2 cans water packed tuna, don't drain

4 egg whites or egg substitute to equal 2 eggs

1 package Mexican cornbread mix, dry

Mix together, make patties and fry in Pam.

OVEN FRIED FISH FILLETS

1 lb. flounder or sole fillets

6 T low-fat bread crumbs

1/2 t paprika

1 T fat-free mayonnaise

2 t dried parsley

Coat fillets with mayonnaise. Combine bread crumbs, parsley and paprika. Dredge coated fillets in bread crumbs mixture. Place fillets on baking sheet sprayed with cooked spray. Bake 450° for 12 minutes or until fillets flake easily with fork.

LEMON SAUCE FOR FISH

1 T cornstarch

1/2 c defatted chicken broth

1 t shredded lemon peel

1 T lemon juice

1/2 c evaporated skim milk

1 t dill weed

Stir cornstarch and lemon juice together until smooth. Stir in milk and broth. Cook and stir over medium heat until thickened and bubbly. Stir in dill weed and lemon peel. Cook and stir on low heat for 2 or 3 minutes more. Serve over fish of your choice.

*"Who satisfies your mouth with good things
so that your youth is renewed like the eagles."*
Psalms 103:5

Poultry

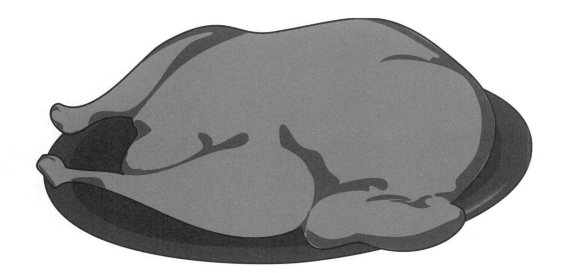

CHICKEN BREASTS
WITH TOMATO & RICE

4 chicken breast, boneless and skinless

2 c Minute Rice

14 1/2 oz. stewed tomatoes (any flavor)

Brown chicken breasts in skillet sprayed with Pam. Add rice and stewed tomatoes, simmer until chicken and rice are done. May need to add a little water for the rice.

Serves 4   Fat: 4 grms per serving

GREEN ENCHILADA CASSEROLE

chicken breast-bone/skinless

cream of chicken soup (Campbell's 97% fat free)

no-fat cheese, grated

chopped onion

green chilis chopped

Guiltless Gourmet Chips

1/2 to 1 can evaporated skim milk

Favorite

Bake or boil chicken breast, cut it up. Mix skim milk with the soup; whisk smooth, add chopped onions, and green chilis. Create a layer of each: chips, chicken, then no-fat cheese. Top with half soup mixture. Now layer again ending with soup or cheese, whichever you prefer. Microwave at full power until thoroughly heated and bubbly.

Serves 1   Fat: 3 grms per serving

POULTRY

CHICKEN A LA DENVER

4 chicken breast, boneless, skinless

3/4 c skim milk

1/2 to 1 whole onion

1 whole diced tomato

Favorite

1 can low-fat cream of
   mushroom soup

1 small can sliced mushrooms

2 cloves minced garlic

Pound chicken breast until thin then cut into 1 inch strips. Sauté onion and chicken until brown in Pam. Mix soup and milk then and add garlic. Pour soup mixture over chicken. Let simmer until nearly done, then add whole diced tomato. Serve over pasta.

SWEET AND SOUR CHICKEN

1 lb. boneless chicken breast, cubed

1 8 oz. can crunched pineapple in juice

1 c carrot strips

1/2 c green pepper strips

1/2 c red pepper strips

1 T cornstarch

3 T brown sugar

1 1/2 c Minute Rice

1/4 c soy sauce

1 garlic clove minced

3 T Vinegar

1/2 t ground ginger

Brown chicken in Pam in a large skillet. Add peppers, carrots, and garlic; cook and stir 1 to 2 minutes. Mix cornstarch and soy sauce. Add to pan with pineapple in juice, vinegar, sugar, and ginger. Bring to a boil. Prepare rice as directed. Serve over rice.

Serves 4   Fat: 3 grms per serving

EASY CHICKEN BAKE

Take boneless, skinless chicken breast. Place in slow cooker. Pour picante sauce over chicken. Add green bell pepper and bake until brown. Serve sauce over baked potato. Add salad and you have a wonderful low-fat meal.

Fat: 3 grms per serving

POULTRY

CHICKEN OR HAM ALFREDO

4 cooked chicken breasts, cut into pieces (can substitute with ham)

1 - 12 oz. package fettuccine noodles

1 8 oz. can sliced mushrooms, drained

1 c evaporated skim milk

4 t fat-free chicken broth

1/3 c fat-free Parmesan cheese

1/4 c flour

1/4 c liquid Butter Buds

1/4 t garlic powder

1/4 t each: pepper and salt

In a sauce pan over low heat, blend flour, Butter Buds, milk, and broth. Add garlic, salt, and pepper. Continue to cook over low heat stirring constantly until sauce thickens. Stir in Parmesan cheese. Combine sauce with chicken and mushrooms, fold into cooked pasta. Serve immediately. Thin sauce with skim milk and chicken broth if necessary.

Serves 8   Fat: 1.9 grms per serving

QUICK CHICKEN SPAGHETTI

1/4 c de-Favoritefatted chicken broth *plus* 1 package Butter Buds 1/4 c green pepper

1 can Campbell's Low-Fat Cream of Mushroom Soup 1/4 c chopped celery

1 small can sliced mushrooms, drained Pam

2 (10 oz.) cans white chicken in water Salt and pepper to taste

1/2 c cheddar cheese, grated

10 oz. pkg. spaghetti, cooked 6 min.

1/4 c chopped green onions

1/2 c fat-free mozzarella cheese, grated

1 t chili powder

Sauté onion, celery and green pepper in broth and Butter Buds about 2 minutes. Add remaining ingredients; mix well. Pour into Pam sprayed casserole; bake at 350° for 20 minutes.

Serves 4 Fat: 8 grms per serving

HONEY DIJON CHICKEN

4 chicken breast boneless, skinless — boil for 5 minutes

Marinate:

Kraft Fat-Free Honey Dijon Dressing

2 - 4 T honey (depending on taste)

1/4 c of water

1 t garlic powder

Dash of salt

1 T pepper

2 t oregano

Favorite

Marinate dry chicken at least 20 minutes, overnight is best if possible. The marinate will be absorbed by the chicken, puffing up the chicken. Bake 10 to 15 minutes at 375°.

Serves 4 Fat: 3 grms per serving

CHEESY CHICKEN FAJITAS

1/2 c red, green and/or yellow pepper strips

1/4 c sliced red onion

1 boneless, skinless chicken breast half, cut into strips

1 T chopped green chilis, drained.

1/8 t ground cumin

1/2 small clove garlic, minced

2 flour tortillas (6 inch)

4 fat-free cheese single

salsa

Spray skillet with cooking spray, sauté onion and peppers until tender. Remove from skillet, spray skillet again and add chicken. Cook until done. Add vegetables, chilis, cumin and garlic, simmer 5 minutes. Place tortilla on microwavable plate, top with cheese, microwave on HIGH 20 seconds. Top with half of chicken mixture, fold sides and serve with salsa.

Serves 2   Fat: 4 grms per serving

CHICKEN FRIED CHICKEN WITH CREAM GRAVY

4 boneless, skinless chicken breasts

2 egg whites, slightly beaten

2 c corn flakes, crushed

salt and pepper

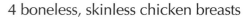
Favorite

GRAVY:

4 T flour

1/2 c evaporated skim milk

2 t Molly McButter

1 c de-fatted chicken broth

1 c skim milk

salt and pepper

Lightly pound chicken breasts with table knife handle until they are thinner, larger and lightly tenderized. Dip in egg white and roll in crushed corn flakes. In skillet sprayed with butter flavored Pam, brown and cook over medium-low heat 5 to 6 minutes on each side (will burn easily) keep heat fairly low. Turn only once. When chicken is done, remove from skillet.

GRAVY: Add flour to skillet, brown over medium heat, stirring occasionally. This will burn easily. Remove from heat and set aside. In medium bowl, combine remaining ingredients. Using a whisk, with skillet still removed from heat, add gravy liquid while stirring. Return to heat, whisk and stir until gravy thickens. Serve gravy spooned over chicken.

Serves 4   Fat: 4 grms per serving

RANCH CHICKEN

4 boneless, skinless chicken breasts

1 oz. pkg. Ranch dressing mix

2 egg whites, slightly beaten

1 c fat-free cheese, shredded

20 fat-free saltines, crushed

Favorite

Preheat oven: 350°. Spray baking sheet with non-stick spray. Dip chicken in egg white, then roll in cheese, then roll lightly in dry Ranch dressing, followed by crackers. Place each chicken breast on baking sheet and bake 35 minutes.

Serves 4　　　　　　　　Fat: 4 grms per serving

CHICKEN CASSEROLE

2 c diced chicken breast

1 1/2 c diced celery

1 c fat-free mayonnaise

1 c fat-free potato chips, crushed

1/2 c water chestnuts, diced

salt & pepper to taste

l/2 c grated cheese

Combine all ingredients except potato chips. Put in Pam sprayed casserole dish. Top with chips. Bake 10 minutes at 450°.

Serves 4 to 6　　　　　　　　Fat: 1.5 grms per serving

CHICKEN WITH CILANTRO SAUCE

2 T lime juice

1 t finely chopped jalapeno

1/2 c nonfat plain yogurt

4 fat-free flour tortillas

1 garlic clove, crushed through a press

4 chicken breasts, about 3 oz. each

1/2 c packed cilantro leaves

2 c Romaine lettuce, cut crosswise
　　in strips

Preheat over to 350°. Combine lime juice, garlic and jalapeno in a bowl. Add chicken, turn to coat and set aside. Process yogurt and cilantro in food processor until smooth. To thicken mixture, refrigerate until ready to use. Warm tortillas in oven or micro and keep warm. In wok or large skillet, brown chicken in Pam and/or fat-free chicken broth, about 1 minute on each side. Place tortilla on a plate, add a layer of shredded Romaine, chicken breast, tomatoes, peppers and a spoonful of cilantro yogurt sauce. Yum Yum!

CHICKEN AND DUMPLINGS

Chicken Broth for Dumplings

4 boneless, skinless chicken breasts

2 cans fat-free chicken broth

3 c water

1 medium chopped onion

1/4 t. garlic powder

1/4 t poultry seasoning

1/2 c chopped celery

salt and pepper

Spray large pot with Pam. Add chicken pieces and brown. Add broth, water, and the rest of the broth ingredients.

Simmer 30 minutes over low heat, uncovered.

DUMPLINGS:

1 c flour

1/2 c no fat cottage cheese

salt to taste

3 egg whites

1\8 c water

DUMPLINGS: Beat combined egg whites and cottage cheese with mixer. Add water, salt and mix well. Add half the flour and mix by hand, mix well, add remaining flour mixing well. Bring chicken broth to a rolling boil. Drop a tablespoon of dough at a time into boiling stock. After all dough has been dropped in, reduce heat, cover and cook for 15 minutes. If a thicker, richer broth is desired uncover and cook longer. Serve sprinkled with Molly McButter.

Serves 8   Fat: 2.2 grms per serving

POULTRY

CHICKEN RICE FIESTA

2 1/2 to 3 lbs. chicken (white meat only)

Salt, black pepper, and paprika

1/4 lb. turkey sausage

3/4 c each diced celery and green onions

3 c cooked rice

1 can whole kernel corn with peppers, undrained

2 t lemon juice

Season chicken with salt, pepper and paproka. Brown in spray release in a large skillet. Remove chicken and set aside. Cook sausage. As you are browning the sausage, add celery and onions, sauté until tender. Add rice, corn, and lemon juice; mix well. Transfer rice mixture to sallow baking dish. Place cooked chicken on top of rice mixture. Cover and bake at 350 degrees for 30 minutes or until chicken is tender. Makes 6 servings.

CAROLYN'S CHICKEN SALAD

4 c cubed cooked chicken breast

1 1/2 c seedless green grapes, halved

1 c chopped celery

3/4 c sliced green onions

3 boiled egg whites

1/2 c fat-free mayonnaise

1/4 c fat-free sour cream

1 T mustard

Salt and pepper to taste

1/4 t onion powder

1/4 t celery salt

1/8 t dry mustard

1/8 t paprika

Favorite

Combine chicken, grapes, celery, onions and egg whites in large bowl. In another bowl, combine the rest of the ingredients; stir until smooth. Pour over the chicken mixture and toss gently.

HAWAIIAN CHICKEN BREAST

1 chicken breast

1/4 c soy sauce

1/2 c crushed pineapple

1/2 bell pepper

3 T brown sugar

Marinate chicken in soy sauce. Place chicken in baking dish. Sprinkle with brown sugar. Pour remaining soy sauce over chicken. Bake covered for 1/2 hour at 350°. Uncover and add pepper and pineapple. Bake 1/2 hour longer.

ROASTED TURKEY

Butterball without skin

Follow poultry producers recommended time and temperature for Roasting. Spray cheesecloth with Pam Butter-Flavored spray - drape over turkey to prevent drying. Add 1 to 2 cups water to roasting pan.

Low Fat: 4.4 grms, Regular Fat: 18.8 grms (oil on cloth) per 4 oz. serving

APPLE-CINNAMON SAUCE FOR TURKEY

1 T Butter Buds or low fat margarine

1 t chicken bouillon

2 T cornstarch

1 1/2 t sugar

1/2 t ground cinnamon

1/4 c finely chopped apples

Melt margarine or heat Butter Buds in medium saucepan. Combine bouillon, cornstarch, sugar, and cinnamon in small bowl. Gradually blend in apple juice. Add juice mixture and apple to butter; cook and stir over medium heat until thickened. Serve over sliced turkey.

Low Fat: .5 grms (Butter Buds), 5 grms. (Low fat margarine)

Regular Fat: 10 grms per serving

TURKEY MEATLOAF

1 lb. ground white turkey breast

1 t Accent

2 Egg Beaters

1 8 oz. tomato sauce

1 1/2 c fat-free wheat crackers

3/4 c ketchup

1 pkg. Lipton Onion Soup Mix

Mix thoroughly. Place in loaf pan sprayed with Pam. Pour tomato sauce over meat mixture. Bake 1 hour at 350°.

Serves 10   Fat: 0.7 grms per serving

"I would have lost heart had I not believed I would see the goodness of the Lord in the land of the living."

Psalms 27:13

Vegetable Dishes

SKILLET FRIED CABBAGE

l/2 head of cabbage   1/2 c chopped onion

1 t bacon bits   1 t Butter Buds (dry)

Heat large skillet with butter flavored Pam. Brown onions and bacon bits. Add cabbage. Cover but stir often, adding a small amount of water as need to prevent burning. Cabbage will cook down. Season with a little amount of salt and pepper. It's great!

Serves 2   Fat: 0.5 grms per serving

FRENCH FRIED ONION RINGS

1 medium onion   1/2 c non-fat yogurt

1 egg white   1 c flour

1 c flour   Dash seasoned pepper

Slice onion and chill in icey water approximately 15 minutes. Drain and separate onions rings, coat with flour, dip in beaten mixture of yogurt, egg white, and seasoned pepper. Recoat with flour. Spread onion rings out on a foil covered cookie sheet sprayed genorously with Pam. Bake at 400° until brown on each side. Broil the last minute to fully cook flour.

Fat: 0 grms per serving

FRIED POTATOES

Boil 3 to 4 medium to large potatoes in skins. Let cool or refrigerate over night for next day. Cut into bite size pieces or wedges. Spray Pam in bottom of non-stick pan. Put potatoes in pan and spray with Pam. Sprinkle with chili powder, salt, pepper, garlic or any flavoring you wish. Heat in oven.

Fat: 0 grms per serving

JEAN'S CHEESY POTATOES

8 c hot boiled potato

2 cartons fat-free French onion dip

1 carton fat-free sour cream

1 8 oz pkg. fat-free cream cheese

3/4 c fat-free grated cheddar cheese

Paprika

Favorite

Whip all ingredients, except grated cheese together. Place in casserole dish. Sprinkle with grated fat-free cheddar cheese and paprika. Heat in oven till heated thoroughly and cheese is melted.

TWICE BAKED POTATOES

4 small baking potatoes

1 carton fat-free sour cream

Salt and pepper to taste

2 T chives

4 oz. fat-free cream cheese

Skim milk

2 T grated Parmesan

1/2 t onion powder, optional

Bake potatoes till tender and slightly cooled. Cut potatoes length wise. Scoop out potato from the skin, leaving a shell. Set shells aside. Add rest of ingredients to the potatoes. Add milk a little at a time, beating until fluffy. Spoon mixtures back into shells. Sprinkle with paprika. Lightly cover with foil and bake 350° degrees for 10 minutes, remove foil and bake 10 more minutes.

HASH BROWN CASSEROLE

VEGETABLES

Hash browns (any brand not pre-fried and fat-free)

Campbell's 97% Fat-Free cream of chicken soup

Fat-free sour cream

Chopped onion

Chopped green chilies

Fat-free grated cheese

Favorite

Mix 1/2 to 1 can skim milk with the soup, blend in 1 cup no-fat sour cream, green chilies and onions. Place a layer of hashbrowns in a microwave dish, cover with cheese and soup mixture. Repeat, ending with cheese on top. Microwave at full power.

Serves 4   Fat: 1 grm per serving

SCALLOPED POTATOES

4 medium potatoes thinly sliced

1 c chopped onions

1 1/2 c skim milk

salt and pepper

fat-free cheese

4 T flour

Layer potatoes in Pam sprayed casserole dish. Dust potatoes lightly with flour, onions layer, and cheese layer. Repeat with potatoes and flour, onions, and cheese until several layers are made. Pour milk over layers and bake until done at 350°.

(Dusting with flour will thicken milk as the potatoes cook. Can also add thinly sliced carrot layer for color.)

Serves 4   Fat: 0 grms per serving

BROCCOLI RICE CASSEROLE

1 small chopped onion

1/2 c evaporated skim milk

2 c cooked rice (white or brown)

8 oz. shredded fat-free cheese

1/2 c chopped water chestnuts

1 can low-fat cream of mushroom soup

1/4 c hot water with 1 chicken bouillon cube and 1 pkg. butter buds

2 (10 oz.) pkgs. frozen chopped broccoli, cooked and drained

1/2 c chopped celery

Pam

1 t garlic salt

dash hot pepper sauce

Sauté onion and celery in butter buds/bouillon mixture in a large skillet until vegetables are crisp-tender. Add broccoli and remaining ingredients; mix well. Pour into a sprayed casserole dish and bake at 350° for 30 minutes or until heated through.

Serves: 10   Fat: 1.5 grms per serving

STEAMED VEGETABLES

Cut bite-sized slices of the following: cauliflower, broccoli, squash, zucchini squash, celery, green pepper, carrots, and onions. Spray large skillet with Pam spray. Add vegetables and stir. Cover, steam and stir often. Salt, pepper, and sprinkle with Butter Buds. (frozen mixed vegetables may be used as desired)

Fat: 0 grms per serving

VEGETABLE CHILI

Favorite

1 can whole kernel corn

1 can Rotel tomatoes

1 can pinto beans

1/2 c Minute Rice

Mix all ingredients in a pan and bring to a boil. Cook 1 minute. Remove from heat and add chili powder (as you like). Cover and let stand until rice is fluffy. (For a milder taste, add a can of chopped tomatoes instead of Rotel tomatoes. Also onion and celery may be added if sautéed first.)

Fat: 0 grms per serving

GREEN BEAN SAUTÉ

4 c whole green beans

1 T + 1 t margarine

1 T + 1 t chopped shallots

1 T + 1 t imitation bacon bits

In large saucepan of boiling water, blanch green beans 3 to 4 minutes or until color intensifies and beans are tender crisp. Drain and reserve. In large non-stick skillet, heat margarine until bubbly. Add shallots and sauté until wilted; stir in bacon bits and reserved beans, toss just until heated through.

Serves 8   Fat: 2 grms per serving

Fat: 0.5 grms per serving (if Ultra Promise, 4 grms fat)

GREEN BEANS ALMONDINE

2 t slivered almonds

2 T snipped fresh dill or 1 1/2 t dillweed

1 T lemon juice

1 t light margarine (1 grms.)

1 lb. green beans, steamed

In a small nonstick skillet, toast the almonds over low heat until lightly browned, shaking the pan occasionally. Remove the almonds from the skillet and set aside. Add the dill, lemon juice and margarine to the skillet. Heat until the margarine is melted. Transfer the beans to a serving bowl. Drizzle with dill mixture and toss. Sprinkle the almonds on top.

Serves: 6   Fat per serving: Low Fat: 0.44 grms, Regular Fat: 4.64 grms per serving

CHILI RELLENOS CASSEROLE

2 (4 oz. cans) chopped green chilis, drained

6-8 oz. fat-free cheddar cheese

1 c frozen egg beaters, thawed

2 c skim milk

1 c no-fat cottage cheese

Favorite

1 c low fat biscuit mix

salsa

Spray two quart baking dish with Pam. Sprinkle cheese and chilis over bottom. Mix together biscuit mix, milk and egg product - beat until smooth. Stir in cottage cheese and spoon over cheese and chilis. Bake, uncovered, 350° for about 45 minutes or until puffed, and knife inserted in center comes out clean. Let stand 10 minutes before serving. Top with hot sauce.

Serves 4   Fat: .5 grms per serving

PASTA STIR FRY

1/2 lb. cooked pasta

1 c diced broccoli

1 c sliced zucchini

cooking spray

1 c sliced mushrooms

1 c onion

2 egg whites

Coat large frying pan with cooking spray. Stir fry onions, mushrooms, broccoli, and zucchini until tender. Toss in pasta, then egg whites, and stir on low until cooked.

Fat: 1 grm per serving

SALLY'S SQUASH CASSEROLE

5 or 6 small yellow squash

1/2 to 1 red and green bell pepper

1/2 c instant potato flakes

1/2 c dry ranch dressing

Egg substitute or egg whites

1/2 to 1 whole onion

1/2 c Parmesan cheese

Slice yellow squash. Mix cheese, potato flakes and dressing in small bowl. Beat egg mixture and put in small bowl. Dip sliced squash in egg substitute or egg whites and then in dry ingredients. Brown slightly in Pam. Add red and green bell peppers, and onion. Pour over all 1/4 cup of water, simmer till tender.

RICE AND SQUASH CASSEROLE

1 1/2 lb. yellow or zucchini, diced

1/2 c chopped onion

3 c cooked rice

2 c grated no fat cheddar cheese

1 t seasoned pepper

1/2 t salt

3 egg whites, slightly beaten

1/2 c fat free mayonnaise

2 T rice flour or all purpose flour

Cook and cover squash and onion in small amount of water in s aucepan until squash is tender but not soft. Drain well. Combine with rice, cheese, pepper, and salt. Blend eggs and mayonnaise; stir into vegetable mixture. Turn into a 2 quart casserole sprayed with vegetable spray release. Top with bread crumbs. Bake at 350 degrees for 30 minutes. Makes 6 servings.

VEGETABLES

CANDIED SWEET POTATOES

4 to 6 baked sweet potatos

1 c Molasses

1/2 c Butter Buds, liquid

1 to 2 c marshmallows

Peel and slice baked potatoes into casserole dish. Top with molasses and Butter Buds. Heat thoroughly in oven, top with marshmallows and brown.

Fat per serving: Low Fat: 1 grm

SWEET POTATO SOUFFLE

1 can (40 oz.) sweet potatoes, drained

1 t grated lemon peel

3/4 t baking powder

1 T Apple juice concentrate

1 t fresh lemon juice

2 T rice flour or all purpose flour

1/3 c powdered/skim milk

1/4 t cinnamon

1 t vanilla extract

2 egg whites

Preheat oven to 325°. Place sweet potatoes in large mixer bowl and beat until smooth. Add remaining ingredients except egg whites; blend until smooth. Beat egg whites in a small mixer bowl with clean beaters on medium speed until stiff but not dry. Fold into potato mixture. Pour into 8" non-stick baking pan and bake uncovered for 50 to 60 minutes until golden brown and set.

Serves 6   Fat: 0 grms per serving

CORN CASSEROLE

1 can cream style corn

1 stick fat-free margarine

1 recipe no-fat cornbread, dry mix only

1 can white kernel corn,
    drain off 1/2 juice

1 carton fat-free sour cream

Combine all ingredients. Mix well. Pour into ungreased pan. Bake at 350° for 1 hour.

BOSTON BAKED BEANS

2 lbs. small white beans

2 T Bac-O's

1/8 c maple syrup

1 t dry mustard

Favorite

1 chopped onion

1/2 c brown sugar

1/8 c molasses

1/2 t black pepper

Simmer beans until tender. Add other ingredients, bake at 325° for 3 hours. Bake last 30 minutes with lid off, but keep moist.

KAREN'S CHILI BEANS

1 small bag beans, cooked

Salt to taste

1 t paprika

2 Bay leaves

1/4 t cayenne pepper

1 large can tomato juice

1 chopped bell pepper

2 heaping t minced onions

3 t chili powder

1 can tomato soup

Cook beans till tender, add the rest of the ingredients and continue cooking till done.

HEARTY BAKED MACARONI

1 16 oz. can tomato puree

2 t Italian seasonings

1 1/2 lbs. fat-free cottage cheese

1 8 oz. pkg. elbow macaroni, uncooked

1 c water

1 t garlic powder

1/2 t onion powder

4 oz. fat free mozzarella cheese, sliced

In a small bowl, combine tomato puree, water, Italian seasonings, and 1/2 teaspoon garlic powder. In another bowl, combine cottage cheese, onion powder, and remaining garlic powder. Spray a 9 x 9 x 2-inch casserole dish with vegetable cooking spray and spread 1/3 of tomato mixture in dish. Layer half the macaroni, all the cheese mixture, and a third of the tomato mixture. Add remaining macaroni and cover with remaining tomato mixture. Cover and bake at 350° F for 1 hour. Uncover and top with mozzarella cheese. Bake uncovered until cheese melts, about 5 min. Let stan for 10 minutes before serving.

"Have you found honey? Eat only as much as you need..."
Proverbs 25:16

Desserts

FAT FREE PINEAPPLE UPSIDE DOWN CAKE

TOPPING:

Pam

2 T Light Karo Corn Syrup

7 pineapple rings (canned)

1/4 c packed brown sugar

1 T. lemon juice

7 marachino cherries

CAKE:

1 c flour

1 1/2 t baking powder

1 c sugar

2 egg whites

1/4 c corn starch

1/2 t salt

2/3 c skim milk

1/3 c Light Karo corn syrup

Preheat oven to 350°. Spray 9" round cake pan with Pam. Add brown sugar, corn syrup, and lemon juice. Stir to combine. Place in oven for 3 minutes. Remove. Arrange pineapple rings and cherries in pan. Set aside. In a large bowl, combine flour, corn starch, baking powder, and salt. In medium bowl, with wire whisk, mix sugar and milk; stir 1 minute. Add egg whites, corn syrup, and vanilla. Stir until well blended. Gradually stir in flour mixture. Spoon batter over pineapple. Bake 35 to 40 minutes or until toothpick is clean. Immediately loosen cake from pan, invert onto serving plate.

Serves 12   Fat: 0 grms per serving

DECADENT FAT-FREE CHOCOLATE CAKE

Pam

1/2 c unsweetened cocoa

1 t baking powder

1 1/4 c sugar

3 egg whites

Favorite

1 1/4 c flour

1/4 c corn starch

1/2 t salt

1 c water

1/2 c Light Karo corn syrup

Preheat oven to 350°. Spray 9 x 9 pan with Pam. In a large bowl, combine flour, cocoa, cornstarch, baking powder and salt. In medium bowl, mix sugar, egg whites, and corn syrup with a wire wisk. Stir in dry ingredients until smooth. Pour into pan. Bake 35 minutes or until toothpick comes out clean. Cool. Sprinkle with powdered sugar if desired.

Serves 16   Fat: 0.5 grms per serving

STRAWBERRY SHORTCAKE

2 pkg. strawberry Jell-O (I use sugar-free)

1 angel food cake

1 large pkg. frozen strawberries

Favorite

Dissolve Jell-O in 2 cups hot water. Add strawberries and stir until dissolved. Place cake in bowl with Jell-O and strawberries. Allow to soak into cake. Refrigerate until ready to serve. Top with low-fat Cool Whip.   Serves 8

JUDY'S ORIGINAL COFFEE CAKE

6 c flour

2 T baking powder

2 t vanilla

Favorite

3 c sugar

5 or 6 c skim milk

Spray 2 9x13 pans with Pam. Mix all together in mixer. Pour batter evenly in both pans. Sprinkle with brown sugar and cinnamon and spray again with Pam. Bake at 350° for 30 min. Drizzle with powder sugar icing.

SURPRISE PEACH COBBLER

1 1/2 c flour

4 t baking powder

1 1/2 c skim milk

1/2 pkg. liquid Butter Buds

1 pkg. Butter Buds, dry

1 c sugar

1/2 c light corn syrup

Pam

4 c fresh sliced, peeled peaches (or 2 (16 oz.) canned peaches without sugar, drained and liquid reserved)

Preheat oven to 350°. Spray Pam on 9 x 13 glass casserole dish and set aside. Mix together flour, baking powder, dry Butter Buds and mix in sugar. Add milk slowly to make the batter. Pour the corn syrup into the casserole dish. Carefully pour batter on corn syrup.(DO NOT MIX OR STIR!!) Spoon peaches gently over the batter keeping a little of the juice, if any, in each spoonful. Pour liquid Butter Buds on top of peaches. Bake 1 hour. Serve with non-fat frozen yogurt if desired.

Note: Add 1/2 - 3/4 cup of sugar to peaches if needed, depending on taste.

Serves 10   Fat: 0.15 grms per serving

CREAMY NEW YORK CHEESECAKE

2 32 oz. cartons plain no-fat yogurt

6 1/4 oz. box Healthy Valley Fat-Free Date Delight cookie, ground into fine crumbs,
about 1 1/2 c (can substitute with graham crackers)

1 c honey

2 t vanilla

5 T arrowroot

5 egg whites

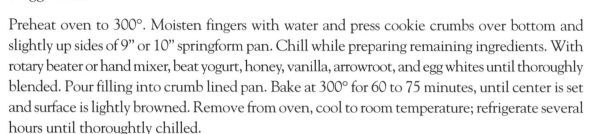

Preheat oven to 300°. Moisten fingers with water and press cookie crumbs over bottom and slightly up sides of 9" or 10" springform pan. Chill while preparing remaining ingredients. With rotary beater or hand mixer, beat yogurt, honey, vanilla, arrowroot, and egg whites until thoroughly blended. Pour filling into crumb lined pan. Bake at 300° for 60 to 75 minutes, until center is set and surface is lightly browned. Remove from oven, cool to room temperature; refrigerate several hours until thoroughtly chilled.

Serves 12   Fat: .3 grms per serving

BREAD PUDDING

1 loaf stale white bread (French is best)

1 c raisins   2 t cinnamon

2 c skim milk   8 egg whites

1 c Mott's natural applesauce   1/2 c brown sugar

1 1/2 t vanilla

Cut bread into 1/2 inch cubes and toss with raisins and cinnamon in a large bowl. Beat together milk, applesauce, egg whites, sugar, and vanilla. Pour custard mixture over bread cubes and let stand 25 minutes. Spray a 9" pan with cooking spray. Pour mixture into prepared pan. Bake for 35-40 minutes at 350° or until knife inserted in center comes out clean. Remove from oven and let stand 15 to 20 minutes before serving. This is great served with lemon sauce made from lemon juice, corn starch, sugar and water.

GINGERBREAD WAFFLES

4 Egg Beaters + 4 egg whites

1/2 c low fat buttermilk (3 grms)

1/2 c low fat margarine (4 grms)

1/2 c light molasses

1/2 c pancake syrup

2 1/4 c all purpose flour

1 1/2 t each ground ginger, cinnamon

1 1/4 t baking soda

1/4 t each ground cloves and nutmeg

1/4 t salt

1 t confectioner's sugar (optional)

Preheat waffle iron according to manufacturer's directions. In large bowl, whisk Egg Beaters together with buttermilk, margarine, molasses, and pancake syrup until smooth. In separate large bowl, with wooden spoon, combine dry ingredients, except salt and confectioner's sugar. Stir dry ingredients into yolk mixture in 3 batches, stirring just until smooth; do not beat. In clean mixer bowl, on high speed, beat whites with salt until stiff but not dry. Stir 1/4 of the whites into yolk and flour mixture; gently fold in remainder. If necessary, spray heated waffle iron with non-stick cooking spray. Spoon 1/4 of the batter (about 1 1/4 cup) into waffle iron and cook according to manufacturer's directions. Remove finished waffles to serving platter; cover loosely with foil and place in low oven to keep warm. Repeat with remaining batter. If desired, before serving, sprinkle with confectioner's sugar.

Serves 8   Fat: 1 grm per serving

Hint: Plain waffles can be made with Pioneer Low-Fat Biscuit Mix for less than .5 grms fat per serving

BLUEBERRY POUND CAKE

1 yellow cake mix

1-8 oz. pkg. fat free cream cheese

1 c canned or frozen blueberries

3 egg substitutes

1/2 c applesauce

Mix egg substitute with cream cheese and applesauce; mix well. Add cake mix and blueberries. Pour into sprayed Bundt pan. Bake at 350° degrees for about an hour, or until done.

DESSERTS

APPLE BROWN BETTY

3/4 c plain, dried low-fat bread crumbs

1/2 c firmly packed light brown sugar

1 t grated lemon rind

1/4 t ground cinnamon

4 small McIntosh apples, pared, cored, and thinly sliced

2 T + 2 t low-fat margarine

1 T fresh lemon juice

Preheat oven to 350°. Spray a 2-quart baking dish with no-stick cooking spray; sprinkle lightly with enough bread crumbs to coat surface; set aside. In small dish, combine sugar, lemon rind, and cinnamon. In prepared dish, layer 1/3 of apples, crumbs, sugar mixture, and dots of margarine; repeat, sprinkling last layer with lemon juice. Bake 40 minutes, until apples are tender.

Serves 8   Fat: 1.5 grms per serving (fat free margarine: 0 grms)

RICE PUDDING WITH RASPBERRY SAUCE

RASPBERRY SAUCE:

3 c frozen unsweetened raspberries, thawed

1/4 c raspberry spread

1/4 c dried currants

1 t vanilla extract

1/2 t ground cinnamon

RICE PUDDING:

2 c skim milk

2 large eggs

1 t grated lemon rind

6 T + 2 t granulated sugar

2 c cooked white rice

1 c evaporated skim milk

2 t vanilla extract

1/8 t ground nutmeg

SAUCE: Combine all (sauce) ingredients in medium saucepan over medium-high heat; cook 6 to 8 minutes, stirring occasionally, until bubbly; refrigerate. Preheat oven to 350°. Spray 2-quart casserole with non-stick cooking spray.

PUDDING: In large bowl, whisk all ingredients except rice until just blended; stir in rice. Pour into casserole. Place casserole in baking pan; add enough hot water to come halfway up side of casserole. Bake 50 minutes, stirring at 20-minute intervals, until almost set in middle. Remove from oven and let stand in waterbath 30 minutes. If desired, sprinkle with additional nutmeg. Serve warm or chilled. On serving plates, spoon 1/8 of sauce around each serving.

Serves 8   Fat: 2 grms per serving (Egg Beaters reduce fat to less than 1 grm)

TRIFLE

1 Angel food cake

1 can pie filling (cherry)

1 sm. vanilla instant pudding

1 Lite Cool Whip

Tear cake into bite size pieces, place in bowl. Set aside. Mix pudding according to directions, using skim milk. Pour over cake. Stir to coat. Pour into serving bowl. Spread pie filling over cake, then spread whipped topping over pie filling.

Serves 10   Fat: .3 grms per serving

PEACH DELIGHT

Favorite

1 can (16 oz.) sliced peaches in light juice

1 pkg. Betty Crocker Super Moist Yellow Cake Mix

1 container (6 oz.) Yoplait Original No-Fat Peach Yogurt (or 2/3 c plain no-fat yogurt)

1 container (4 oz.) frozen low-fat whipped topping, thawed

Heat oven to 350°. Spray 2 round cake pans with Pam. Drain peaches, reserving juice. Add enough water to reserved juiceto measure 1 1/4 cups. Prepare cake mix as directed on package, except substitute juice mixture for the water, and 2 egg whites for l egg. Pour batter into pans. Bake and cool as directed. Cut peaches into bite-size pieces. Mix yogurt and whipped topping. Fold in peaches. Fill layers with about half of the peach mixture. Spoon remaining peach mixture over top of cake. Refrigerate about 2 hours or until chilled.

Serves 10   Fat: .3 grms per serving

ANGEL CHOCOLATE & RASPBERRY DREAM

1/2 small angel food cake

3 c skim milk

1 large pkg. vanilla sugar-free instant pudding

1 c fresh or frozen raspberry

4 T fat free chocolate topping

Use 8" square glass baking dish. Cut 1/2 of the angel food cake and cut in half again. Using 1/4 of the cake, break into bite size pieces and make a layer of cake pieces in the bottom. Sprinkle 1 cup raspberries over the pieces of cake. Prepare instant pudding according to package directions, except, beat only until mixture starts to thicken. Immediately pour half over cake bits. Drizzle 2 tablespoons chocolate topping over pudding. Using the 1/4 cake that is left, break into pieces and make another layer. Pour on remaining pudding and drizzle 2 more tablespoons of chocolate over top. Chill for at least 20 minutes before serving.

Serves 6   Fat: 0 grms per serving

DESSERTS

ORANGE & PINEAPPLE RICE PUDDING

1 c rice (not instant)

1/4 c sugar

1/2 c evaporated skim milk

1 8 oz. can crushed pineapple

1/2 c orange juice

1 c skim milk

1 t orange peel

1/4 t salt

Preheat oven 350°. In medium saucepan combine all ingredients and stir over medium heat until sugar is dissolved. Spray a medium sized, deep casserole dish with non-stick cooking spray. Pour mixture into casserole dish and cover and bake for 1 hour. After one hour, remove lid and return to oven to cook uncovered for 15 minutes more. Can serve either warm or cold, it's delicious either way!

Serves 4   Fat: 0 grms per serving

BANANA MALLOW PIE

8 oz. non-fat cream cheese

1 small pkg. sugar-free vanilla pudding

1 3/4 c non-fat milk (made from dry milk)

Butter Buds, liquid (enough so you can press in pan)

1 1/2 c small marshmallows

2 bananas, sliced

9 crushed graham crackers

Crush and press graham crackers in pie pan, using liquid Butter Buds. Blend cream cheese and vanilla pudding with milk, until smooth. Fold in marshmallows. Place bananas on top of crust. Pour on pudding mixture. Top with Dream Whip made with non-fat milk. Chill and serve.

Serves 8   Fat: 1 grm per serving1/2 t ground cinnamon

PEACH RICE PUDDING

2 1/2 c cooked rice

2 1/2 c skim milk

1/3 c sugar

1 t vanilla

1/4 c honey

2 T fat free margarine

2 t lemon juice

1/2 t grated lemon peel

1/3 t nutmeg

1/8 t salt

1 can diced peaches in juice, drained or 1 1/2 c sliced fresh peaches

Combine rice, milk, and sugar, cook over medium heat in 3 quart sauce pan until hick and creamy, about 20 to 25 minutes stirring often. Add vanilla. Pour into serving dish. Heat honey, butter, lemon juice, lemon peel, nutmeg, and salt. Stir in drained peaches, cook over low heat about 10 minutes. Spoon over rice pudding. Serve warm or cool.

SUGAR FREE-FAT FREE APPLE PIE

1 c Grape-Nuts cereal

3 medium apples

3 T frozen apple juice concentrate

2 T lemon juice

1/2 t cinnamon

Mix cereal with 3 T apple juice. Pack in layers in no-stick tart pan. Sprinkle crust with 1/4 teaspoon cinnamon. Arrange apples and sprinkle with lemon juice and 1/4 teaspoon cinnamon. (I add 4 pkgs. of Equal.) Cover with foil and bake at 350° for 45 minutes. Cool to room temperature.

Combine 1 tablespoon corn starch, 1/2 cup water, and 1/2 cup apple juice concentrate. Cook until thick and clear. Brush over apples. Chill.

Serves 8   Fat: 0 grms per serving

PECAN PIE

3/4 c Egg Beaters

1 tsp vanilla

2 pkg. butter buds + 1/3 c water

3/4 c Light Karo corn syrup

1/2 c sugar

pie crust (9") (see recipe, page 77)

2 T flour

1 tsp vinegar

1/4 c Dark Karo corn syrup

1 c Grape Nuts

Mix all ingredients well. Pour into prepared pie crust. Bake at 375° for 10 minutes. Reduce 350° and bake until top is brown and filling is set.

Serves 8   Fat: 0.9 grms per serving

DESSERTS

PUMPKIN PIE - 1 GRAM OF FAT

1 unbaked 9-inch deep dish pie crust (see recipe)

Pumpkin filling

1 16 oz. can pumpkin

2 Egg Beaters or any fat-free real egg product

3/4 c granulated sugar

1/2 t salt

2 t pumpkin pie spice (cinnamon, nutmeg, allspice, and ginger)

1 c evaporated skim milk

Preheat oven 425°. Mix pumpkin pie ingredients, pour in pie shell and bake 15 minutes. Reduce heat to 325° for 30 to 40 minutes or until done in center.

Serves 8   Fat: 0 grms, Regular Fat: 3 grms per serving

PIE CRUST

1 c Pioneer Low-Fat biscuit mix

1/2 c flour

1 t Molly McButter

I T sugar

5 to 6 T cold water

Prepare pie crust. Mix together biscuit mix, flour, Molly McButter, and sugar. Blend 3 tablespoons water to mixture, adding 1 teaspoon more at a time until slightly moist. Knead dough slightly. Spray two sheets wax paper with Pam. Place ball of dough in center between wax papers. Roll out pie crust to approximately 12 inches. Very carefully peel top sheet of wax paper off pie crust. Place pie crust in Pam sprayed pie pan, wax paper up. Very carefully peel wax paper off pie crust. Spraying fingers will aide in separating pie crust from wax paper. Double edges with extra pie crust and pinch (creating whatever edge you like). Spray crust edges with Pam. Pie crust edges will bake up hard but the crust under pie filling will be tender. Make a tent of foil around edge of pie to prevent the edges from burning.

Hint: For baked pie crust, the pie crust will be hard when baked, but will soften when filling is added.

Fat: 0 grms, Regular Fat: 15 grms per serving

CORN FLAKE PIE CRUST

3 c corn flakes, crushed

2 T sugar

1 1/2 T fat-free cream cheese

Grind corn flakes in food processor, add sugar and process just enough to mix. Add half of cream cheese and process. Add remaining cream cheese and process. Spray 9" pie plate with non-stick cooking spray. Pour in crust mixture. Gently and evenly press to bottom and sides to form crust. Chill before adding filling.

Fat: Less than 1 grm per serving

LITE 'N' DREAMY

2 pkg. mixed fruit Jell-O

1 c peach juice (drained from can)

1 carton fat-free peach yogurt

2 c boiling water

1 can sliced peaches

Stir boiling water into Jell-O in bowl until completely dissolved. Stir in peach juice. Then add yogurt and peaches. Chill about 2 hours.

Serves 4   Fat: 0 grms per serving

TROPICAL FRUIT BRUNCH PARFAIT

1 can (15 1/4 oz.) Dole tropical fruit salad

1 c fat-free cottage cheese

1 carton (8 oz.) no-fat, sugar-free peach yogurt

1/2 c fat-free, plain granola

1/4 c raisins

Drain tropical fruit salad. Combine cottage cheese, yogurt, and raisins. Layer into 4 glasses: Cottage cheese mixture, fruit salad, and granola.

Serves 4   Fat: 0 grms per serving

DESSERTS

FRUIT PIZZA PARTY TRAY

1 Pillsbury Sugar Cookie dough roll

1 fat-free cream cheese spread

1 small jar apricot preserves

1/3 c brown sugar

Assorted fruit

Roll sugar cookie dough onto Pam sprayed pizza pan. Cook as package direction. Cool, then spread with cream cheese and brown sugar. Top with diced or sliced fruit. Heat preserves, and drizzle over fruit. Slice into servings. (Fat content according to package of sugar dough.)

Approximately 20 servings Fat: 4.5 grms per serving for 18 servings.

APRICOT CANDY

1 lb. dried apricots, chopped fine

juice of one orange (approximately 8 T)

2 c sugar

Mix ingredients in a sauce pan, bring to a medium boil. Boil 10 minutes. Stirring constantly, remove from heat. Stir in 3/4 - 1 cup grapenuts. Drop on wax paper. Let cool. Roll in sugar. (Can also use apples, 16 tablespoons orange Juice, 1 teaspoon applepie spices cook the same.)

Fat: 0 grms per serving

CHOCOLATE CARAMEL BARS

2 Egg Beaters

1/2 c Kraft Fat-Free Miracle Whip

1 t vanilla

2 c flour

1 cup fat-free fudge topping

3/4 c sugar

3/4 c brown sugar

1 t baking soda

1/2 c fat-free caramel topping

1 c Grape Nuts Cereal

Heat oven 350°. Cream together Egg Beaters, sugars, Miracle Whip, and vanilla at medium speed with electric mixer; add flour and baking soda. Set aside 1 cup of batter. Spread remaining batter into a 13" x 9" baking dish that has been sprayed with a low-fat cooking spray. Bake 12 to 15 minutes or until lightly browned. Cool 10 minutes. Spread caramel and fudge topping over the crust. Sprinkle Grape Nuts over this. Spoon reserve 1 cup batter over the Grape Nuts. Continue baking 12 to 15 minutes or until lightly browned. Cool. Cut into squares. These can be served alone as cookie bars, or warm with fat-free ice cream or no-fat frozen yogurt on top for a delicious dessert.

Serves 36   Fat: 0.1 grms per serving

D
E
S
S
E
R
T
S

CHOCOLATE SQUARES

3/4 c flour

1/3 c cornstarch

1/2 t salt

2 egg whites

3/4 c applesauce

1 t vanilla

Favorite

1/3 c cocoa

1 t baking powder

2/3 c sugar

1/2 c evaporated skim milk

1/2 c corn syrup

Mix all ingredients together and bake at 350° 35 to 40 minutes.

ICING

1 1/2 c confectioner's sugar

2 T cocoa

Water as needed

Fat: .5 grms per serving

1/2 t vanilla

1 T skim milk

NO GUILT BROWNIES

3 oz. unsweetened chocolate, chopped

1 c granulated sugar

3/4 c flour

3/4 c fat-free cottage cheese

3 egg whites

1 t vanilla

powdered sugar

For variation, I often add 1 t cinnamon.
Heat oven to 350 degrees. Over very low heat, melt chocolate, cool slightly. In food processor or blender, puree all ingredients except chocolate and powdered sugar until smooth. Add melted chocolate and blend well. Pour into sprayed 8 inch square pan. Bake 20 to 30 minutes or just until set. Sprinkle with powdered sugar. Cut into squares.

MOCK SWEETENED CONDENSED MILK

3/4 c sugar

2 1/4 c instant non-fat dry milk

1/2 c water

1/2 t vanilla

Mix, heat, and stir to dissolve.

Fat: 0 per serving (New-Eagle Brand Low-Fat condensed milk - 1.5 grms. per serving)

DESSERTS